How to Rock Your Baby

. . .

ALSO BY ERIN BRIED

How to Sew a Button
How to Build a Fire

How to Rock Your Baby

And Other Timeless Tips for Modern Moms

. . .

Erin Bried

HYPERION

New York

The recommendations and suggestions in this book are not intended to replace the advice given to you by your physician or other health professionals. All matters regarding your pregnancy, health, and childcare should be discussed with your doctor. Before using any herbal remedies or vitamins mentioned in this book, be sure to consult with the appropriate health professionals and check the products' labels for any warnings or cautionary notes. Keep in mind that herbal remedies and supplements are not as strictly regulated as drugs.

The author and publisher disclaim any liability directly or indirectly from the use of the material in this book by any person.

Library of Congress Cataloging-in-Publication Data

Bried, Erin.
How to rock your baby : and other timeless tips for modern moms / Erin Bried. — 1st ed.
p. cm.
ISBN 978-1-4013-2459-9
1. Child rearing.   2. Mother and child.   3. Parenting.   I. Title.
HQ769.B6748 2012
649'.1—dc23
2011051296

Hyperion books are available for special promotions and premiums. For details contact the HarperCollins Special Markets Department in the New York office at 212-207-7528, fax 212-207-7222, or email spsales@harpercollins.com.

Illustrations and book design by Simon M. Sullivan

FIRST EDITION

10 9 8 7 6 5 4 3 2 1

THIS LABEL APPLIES TO TEXT STOCK

FOR ELLIE ROSE

Contents

· · ·

2 · Delivering

3 · Nourishing

4 · Comforting

5 · Polishing

6 · Making

7 · Relating

8 · Surviving

9 · Enjoying

10 · Remembering

Introduction

...

Last year, when I was pregnant for the first time (and, let's just say, a little nervous about the whole thing), I read absolutely every motherhood-, pregnancy-, and baby-related book I could get my hands on. And then, when I finished those, I Googled just about every motherhood-, pregnancy-, and baby-related topic I could think of. Had you checked the search history of my computer, you would've seen I was a woman obsessed. I was about to take on the most important role of my life, and I wanted to give my baby the best I could.

As my belly grew, so did my concerns. For instance, I'd learned that bumpers, those fluffy, quilted numbers parents once lined the crib with, were now considered suffocation hazards. But what about the newfangled, breathable, mesh ones? I remember sitting in my ob-gyn's office sometime during my third trimester, and after asking her a litany of questions, which yes, I wrote down beforehand, I finished, somewhat breathlessly, with, "OK, last one: What do you think about the new breathable bumpers?" She smiled at me, kindly, and said, "Well, I'm not sure. I do know that I've never heard of a baby who has been seriously injured from sticking her arm out of her crib. Wouldn't she just pull it back in?"

As you may be able to tell, my head was absolutely spinning from all the research I'd done. As you may also be able to tell, all that research didn't help me all that much, mainly because the advice varied so greatly from book to book. One would say, whatever you do, never let your baby cry, while the next would say, once she's old enough, you must let her cry it out at night. One would say, wash your hands every time you even think about your baby, while another would say, exposure to germs will make him stronger. One would say, if you allow a single drop of formula to pass through your child's lips, her digestive system will be forever ruined, while another would say, formula is an absolute lifesaver.

In my hormonal fog, I'd lie awake at night, propped up by a million pillows, wondering, Is there any possible way I won't screw this up?

So, confused as ever, I did what any anxious mother-to-be would do: I went to visit my own mom, a kindergarten teacher and grandmother, who lives a hundred miles away from me, in Pennsylvania. She spent a long afternoon walking me through an overwhelmingly large baby store, where she helped me pick out everything I needed, from crib sheets to a car seat, as well as a few things I never even knew I needed (or ever wanted to know about), like nipple cream and butt paste. While we were strolling through the aisles, she told me not to worry so much. "I used to fill your bottle with apple juice and put you to bed," she confessed. "We all did. It's a wonder any of you have teeth at all."

Particularly after reading so many books that took such a staunch position on what's right and wrong, it would've been easy to be horrified by her confession. *Babies don't need all that sugar!* But after we left the store, we spent time with my young nieces, her granddaughters, who love her to the moon and back. Watching her with them, I realized that while parenting trends may indeed change from generation to generation, and even year to year, there are some things that just don't. Some things are truly timeless.

So when I got back home to Brooklyn, I set aside the books, turned off my computer, and waddled off on a mission to learn the parenting lessons that have stood the test of time. And I figured, who better to ask than extraordinary mothers, who've raised extraordinary children? I tapped women from all over the country, from ages 39 to 102, and posed the same doozy of a question to each of them: How did you do it? Hearing their stories, I found not only real practical advice, but also comfort, compassion, and, perhaps most importantly, a dose of newfound confidence.

I sat with 102-year-old Betty Horton in her summer cottage on the shores of Lake Erie. She told me that she had her first daughter at age 24, and her second soon after. "I was happy," she says, "but I was kind of scared, too." World War II broke out when both of her girls were still very young, and her husband joined the navy, leaving her alone to raise them, while he fought in Europe and the South Pacific for the next four years. When I expressed surprise and admiration, Horton brushed it off. "I got through it," she said. "I just did, because I had to." (Later, when I mentioned that I was taking prenatal yoga, she brushed that off, too. "I think that's a bunch of hooey," she said.) What she remembered more clearly than the worry or the sleepless nights was the song she used to sing to her girls. That afternoon on her porch, she sang it to me with tears in her eyes: "Come, little leaves/ Said the wind one day; Come to the meadows/With me and play. Put on your dresses/Of red and gold; For summer is past/And the days grow cold."

I also spent an afternoon in Brooklyn with Erinn McGurn, who, at thirty-nine, is the youngest mother I interviewed. Her twins were born so prematurely, at thirty weeks, that they had to spend the first three months of their lives in the Neonatal Intensive Care Unit. No mother would hope that her babies would have to struggle so much just to survive from the moment they were born, and yet that was McGurn's reality. "I was in combat mode," she says of the time. "I had to keep it together, because I was responsible for them, and I wouldn't do them any good by falling apart." She discovered strength she never knew she had, and with her steady support, her children grew ounce by ounce. Now they're happy, healthy, and rambunctious three-year-olds. At first glance, you'd never know they had such a hard beginning, but look a little closer, and you'll notice something powerful within both of them. Seeing them play at the park with their mother, I know exactly where they got it.

A number of the other mothers I interviewed have raised children who've made it to the very top of their fields. I wanted to know what they did to inspire their kids to reach for the stars. Sunchita Tyson, mother of astrophysicist Neil DeGrasse Tyson, recognized her son's interest in space early on and encouraged him to work hard and save his money to buy his first telescope. Christine Samuel, mother of two-time Super Bowl winner Asante, noticed her son's speed as soon as he could walk, and after she signed him up for football, she never missed a game. Cellist Ruth Alsop, mother of Marin, the first female conductor of a major American orchestra, immersed her daughter in a world of music even before she was born. When Marin expressed an interest in playing, she encouraged her to not only join the orchestra but also to lead it. Elaine Maddow, mother of Rhodes scholar and MSNBC host Rachel, said that her daughter was born with an inherent sense of curiosity. "Even as a baby, Rachel arrived with a real quizzical look on her face, wanting to check everything out," she says, adding that they spent many family dinners talking about the world beyond their front door. "Even now, when I watch her on TV, I still see that very same look." Rose Giunta, mother of Medal of Honor winner Salvatore, says he was strong-willed from the start, and she taught him to use his power to fight for what's right. "We always wanted our children to know that they could make a difference," she says. Esther Safran Foer, mother of authors Franklin, Jonathan, and Joshua, summed it up this way: "From the moment they're born, children are individuals. They have different strengths and weaknesses. So it's your job, as their mother, to find the good and praise it."

For more perspective, I turned to Mary Huff, who is not famous in any way but is certainly a star to her family—her very, *very* large family. I know that whenever I feel overwhelmed by the prospect of raising one child, I'll think of Huff, who has raised not only four of her own, plus four adopted children, but also, through the years, more than thirty foster children, too. In talking to her, I learned that a mother's job is closer to that of a shepherd than anything else. "I think you have to show them values and teach them manners and then you kind of let them do things on their own. They have to learn," she says. When I asked her for her single best piece of advice for me, or any new mom, she replied, "For sure, love 'em. Beyond that, everything else is just gravy."

That brings me back to my own mom, who told me something similar. She said, "If you're loving, nurturing, and caring, everything else will fall into place."

And you know what? It did. In March of 2011, I gave birth to a beautiful baby girl. She spent the first hour of her life staring into my eyes, and in those precious moments, everything unimportant just fell away. Somehow from the time I started writing this book to now, she's learned to crawl and is even taking her first wobbly steps. And I know that when I look back on this time, I won't remember which stroller was supposedly best, but I will remember her first belly laugh, which came during a bath when she discovered her ability to make a splash. I won't remember which brand of pacifier we used, but I will remember the intensity and sloppiness of her first kiss, which landed squarely on my nose. I won't remember whether I ultimately used those breathable bumpers in her crib, but I will remember rocking her in my arms at four o'clock in the morning and singing her to sleep with this song: "May the long time sun shine upon you. All love surround you. And the pure light within you, guide your way on." By the way, I learned that song in my prenatal yoga class. It turns out it wasn't all hooey after all.

If you're expecting now, I hope that this collection of tips will help you rest at least a little bit easier. But above all, know this: You'll find your own way. Sooner than you realize, you're going to be walking down the street with your little one in tow and you'll see an exhausted, slightly frazzled, possibly terrified-looking new mom out with her newborn, who somehow looks tinier and more fragile than you remember yours ever being. You'll smile at this mother and ask her how old her baby is, and she'll respond with a number, measured in weeks, not months or years. And that's when you'll realize that you're on the other side. You'll look at her and give her this timeless advice: "Enjoy it. It goes by so fast." And she won't understand, but that's OK, because you do.

Meet the Mothers
...

It's my great pleasure to introduce you to these ten extraordinary mothers, all of whom contributed their stories and wisdom to this book.

Ruth Alsop

Ruth Alsop was born into a large Irish Catholic family on February 24, 1931, in Melrose, Massachusetts. Her father, who worked in the insurance business before joining the army, and her mother expected only the best of her and her four siblings, and Alsop delivered. She took up the cello, and after graduating from Juilliard, she earned a seat in the orchestra at Radio City Music Hall. In 1955, she married a violinist and soon became pregnant. "I played four shows a day," she says of her exhausting schedule during her pregnancy, "and then I'd go upstairs and sleep in the Rockettes' beds." In 1956, she gave birth to her only child, a daughter named Marin, in a harrowing delivery. "They couldn't stop the bleeding," says Alsop. "I just remember seeing my husband in the hallway, and he kissed me in front of everybody, and I thought, Oh I must be pretty far gone, if you're doing this. Then, I woke up when they were giving me the last rites." Of course, this story has a happy ending: Mother and baby pulled through, and

Alsop, who later spent forty-five years playing in the New York City Ballet orchestra, immersed her daughter in music. "I wanted to share my life with her," she says, adding that Marin took up violin at age six and, after graduating from Yale and Juilliard, eventually joined the New York City Ballet orchestra to play alongside her parents. In 2007, Marin was appointed the director of the Baltimore Symphony Orchestra, making her the first female conductor of a major American orchestra. In the meantime, she also founded Orchkids, a program which helps introduce underprivileged children to classical music, as well as a mentoring program for young female conductors. "Marin is very strong-willed, and I think she got a lot of that from me, and I got my strength from my mother, and I expect that she got hers from her own mother," says Alsop, adding, "It's there in all of us. It just has to be recognized and nourished."

Claire Bried

Claire Bried, my mother, was born on May 13, 1947, in Bangor, Pennsylvania. After losing her father to cancer at age nine, she was raised with her older brother by her mother, who worked in the local courthouse and taught piano lessons to make ends meet. "I never felt like we were doing without," says Bried, now a kindergarten teacher. "My mom was so strong and also so funny, and because of that, I always wanted to be like her." In 1970, after graduating from Penn State, Bried married a naval officer, and the young couple was soon stationed overseas in Rota, Spain. Bried remembers the day she found out she was pregnant with her first daughter. "The doctor had called me with the results of my pregnancy test in the morning, and that night, there was a formal navy ball. I wore the gown I wore in my college roommate's wedding, and I told Dad the good news when we were dancing. He just hugged and kissed me." Upon returning stateside, Bried gave birth to two more daughters, including me, and dedicated her life to making ours better. "Because I came from such a small family," she says, "I knew I wanted to create a bigger one for myself." When I asked her how she knew that she had enough love to go around, she said, "The love is always there. It just comes. You don't know where it comes from, but it's always there."

Rosemary Giunta

Rosemary Giunta, of Hiawatha, Iowa, was born on March 22, 1958, and married her husband, Steve, a medical equipment technician, in 1981. Over the next ten years, she gave birth to two sons, Salvatore and Mario, and a daughter, Katie. A stay-at-home mom, Giunta wanted to be the one to instill values in her children. "It was either I'd teach them or the world would, and I was pretty sure I wanted to do it," says Giunta. "I wanted them to respect all people. And if they saw something that wasn't right, I wanted them to be a voice, to speak up. I always told them, 'If you see somebody getting bullied, you go in there and help. And if you get knocked down, come home, I'll bandage you up, and go back out there and do it again if you have to.'" The message especially resonated with her oldest, Sal, who after high school enlisted in the army and served two tours in Afghanistan. On the night of October 25, 2007, Sal, then twenty-two, was on a mission in the Korengal Valley in northeast Afghanistan with his platoon. While traveling single-file along a rocky ridge, they were ambushed. Sal was fourth in line, and after the first three men were shot, he ran into enemy fire to drag his nearest buddy to safety. Though a bullet hit his body armor, and another his gun, he, along with the rest of his platoon, charged ahead, until they reached the second injured soldier. While the other soldiers tended to that soldier's wounds, Sal continued on alone, over the crest of the hill, only to see his best friend's limp body being dragged away by Taliban fighters. Sal sprinted toward them, killing one of them, wounding the other, and recovering his friend. He spent the next half hour trying to save the life of Sergeant Joshua C. Brennan, who died the next day while in surgery. On November 16, 2010, President Obama presented Sal with the Medal of Honor, the highest possible distinction for military service. Says Giunta, "I'm proud, because I know Sal stood up for something good and right. That's what my husband and I wanted the kids to get. We never wanted them to walk away and shake their heads and say, 'I can't make a difference.'"

Betty Horton

At 102 years old, Betty Horton is one of the oldest mothers in America, which means she has more perspective on the matter than nearly anyone else. She was born in Conneaut, Ohio, on September 7, 1909. "I was raised in the roaring twenties, and we always had a good time," she says, adding, "We lived through prohibition, and given some of the stuff we drank, I'm surprised we lived through the evening." In 1933, at age twenty-three, she married Miles Horton, and a nearly scandalous twelve months later, Diane, her first daughter, was born. "Everyone was terribly surprised. My mother took me to the doctor, who was this gruff old guy, and when I told him I'd missed my period, he scared the wits out of me! I cried. His nurse, who, I'll never forget, was named Miss Pain, said to me, 'He never had a baby. He doesn't know.'" Six years later, after suffering two miscarriages, Horton gave birth to her second daughter, Karen. About a year later, over Christmas, her husband sat her down for a talk. "He said, 'Well, I have something to tell you, and you're not going to do anything about it. I've enlisted in the Seabees.' That's the construction battalion, and they're all overseas. I felt bad naturally, but there was nothing I could do. If I'd raised Cain, he would've been angry at me the rest of his life, because he wanted to go." Miles was gone for the next four years, participating in both the invasion of France and the Battle of Okinawa. "We managed," says Horton, who relied on her mother and mother-in-law for support, while also rolling bandages and knitting washcloths for the war effort. "We had to because there was no choice." She carried that common sense can-do philosophy through her entire life as a parent. "I know I was no bouquet of roses to live with, but I loved my little babies. To be a good parent, it takes love and understanding, and beyond that, you just try. What else can you do? You do the best you can."

Mary Huff

Mary Huff was born on August 4, 1942, in Erie, Pennsylvania, where her father owned a grocery store and her mother stayed at home to care for her and her three younger brothers. At age thirteen, Huff met the love of her life at church, and the two married a year after graduating from high school. In 1962, at age twenty, she gave birth to her first of four children, three sons and a daughter, who would come over the next nine years. "Some girls went to college, but I never wanted that. I wanted to get married and have kids," says Huff proudly. "I've just always wanted to be a mom." Meanwhile, a local judge had begun a program called Volunteers in Probation, which paired troubled teenage boys with loving families, and Huff agreed to participate. "We thought if you could help children, that'd be a good thing. We just felt we needed to, because we always believed you should leave the world better than you found it." Though it was, of course, trying at times, she and her husband enjoyed the experience so much that they opened their hearts and home to even younger children in need. Over the years, Huff became a mother, if only temporarily, to about thirty-six foster children, and between 1981 and 1985, she adopted four of them, a son and three daughters. "All kids need is somebody to love them," she says. This past year, Huff celebrated her fiftieth wedding anniversary with her husband, and all of her children, biological and adopted, as well as many of her foster children, joined in the celebration, toasting the happy couple. Of her role as a mother, she says, simply, "It's a wonderful thing." And there are about forty grown children out there who would certainly agree.

Elaine Maddow

Elaine Maddow was born on June 16, 1941, in Newfoundland, Canada, and raised in a very strict Catholic household, with her seven siblings, by her mother and fisherman father. "All I ever saw my mother do with eight children was work hard, so I thought well maybe I would just not do that," says Maddow, who now lives in Castro Valley, California. "I'd be a career lady or sail the seas or do something really different." In the fall of 1968, she married, and on July 11, 1969, she gave birth to her son, David, now associate director of a legal search consulting firm. "It wasn't really planned, but he was such a great kid and we enjoyed him so much that we decided to have another." Her daughter, Rachel Maddow, who arrived on April 1, 1973, went on to earn her doctorate in political science at Oxford University in England, which she attended on a Rhodes Scholarship, and eventually to host her own Emmy Award–winning television program, *The Rachel Maddow Show*, on MSNBC. "I definitely was not a type of mother who got out of my kids' way and let them explore on their own," says Maddow. "But my children were so smart and so independent that they made their own way in spite of me, especially Rachel." Maddow, a school program administrator and former kindergarten teacher, always taught her children to stand up for what they thought was right and change what they thought was wrong. "There was a lot of discussion of fairness in our house," she says. "At dinner, we'd ask them, 'What went right and what went wrong in your day?' And we discouraged whining. That was a big deal. If they whined, we'd say, 'Whining is not going to do a thing. Now, how are you going to take care of it?'" She's proud of the adults her children have become. "They're good people and good citizens. They're passionate and smart and they care about other people and the world. And who would've ever thought we'd wind up with Rachel being in the position she's in. I really believe in her and what she's doing. She's really my hero."

Erinn McGurn

Erinn McGurn was born on December 4, 1972, in Rowland Heights, California, and raised outside of San Francisco, with her older brother, by her mother, a customer service manager, and father, who worked in a grocery store. The first to finish college in her family, McGurn graduated from Smith, went on to the University of Texas at Austin, where she obtained her master's degree in architecture, and eventually settled in Brooklyn. In 2003, she married Guy Baron, a research analyst who was born in Zimbabwe and raised in Israel, and the two traveled the world together. After touring a crumbling school in Zambia in 2006, they founded Scale Africa, a not-for-profit dedicated to building sustainable schools in sub-Saharan Africa. In February 2008, McGurn became pregnant with twins. Early contractions, gestational diabetes, and eventually pre-eclampsia complicated her pregnancy, and on August 17, just thirty weeks after she conceived, she had to deliver her babies. Her son, Alexander, weighed 3 pounds 4 ounces. Her daughter, Talia, weighed a mere 1.5 pounds and measured 12.5 inches long. "I didn't know if they'd make it," says McGurn, who for the next three months spent fifteen hours a day by their sides in the Neonatal Intensive Care Unit. "All of a sudden, I was a mom, and the *only* thing I was allowed to do was hold them. That was *all* I could do, and so that's what I did." By late fall, Alex and Talia had each reached four pounds, and McGurn was finally able to bring them home, where they've thrived ever since. "Seeing them grow and change has been the most rewarding," she says. "When they turned three, we got them little bicycles with training wheels. At first, they couldn't push the pedals. They couldn't get the mechanics of it. But twenty minutes later, Talia was zooming around! I cried. I call her my little baguette, because that's how big she was. To see that little person who struggled so much master something . . . Certain things just come easy to her, and I feel like she deserves that. When they figure something out themselves, it's amazing to see. They're tiny little evolving things all the time."

Esther Safran Foer

In 1946, Esther Safran Foer was born in Germany, in a displaced-persons camp, where she spent the first three years of her life. Her parents were Holocaust survivors. "I grew up without grandparents, aunts, and uncles, and my parents had very little," she says, adding that despite these circumstances, "I had a happy childhood. I didn't know there were other ways to live, and I was *adored* by my parents. The children born at that time, we were the reaffirmation of life." Her family, including her younger brother, soon moved to Washington, D.C., where her father ran a grocery store before dying roughly four years later. Safran Foer credits her mother with her strength. "My mother was incredibly positive, and she had so much energy and determination, which is probably why she survived the war. Her determination made us who we are to this day." Safran Foer attended the University of Maryland and did some graduate work at Boston University, and in 1971, she married. The following year, she served as the Illinois state press secretary for Democratic presidential candidate George McGovern. In 1974, she gave birth to her first son, Franklin. "I knew I was pregnant with him the next morning," says Safran Foer, who was so excited that she wanted to immediately share the news with everyone in her family. "At Thanksgiving, I did. I hadn't even gone to the doctor for confirmation yet! Later, when I did go to the doctor, he said, 'No, you're not pregnant.' I said, 'I *know* what's going on. Try again.' He did, and I was. It turned out he just had a bad test the first time." In 1977 and 1982, she had two more sons, Jonathan and Joshua. Safran Foer says her biggest challenge as a mother was recognizing her children's individuality, though they each clued her in the moment they were born. "Frank was easygoing and gentle. Jonathan was strong-willed.

And I saw Joshua come out with a look like 'I want to see what the world is like! I'm looking around and taking it all in.'"

Today, all three of her sons are writers: Franklin is an editor at large for the *New Republic* and author of *How Soccer Explains the World: An Unlikely Theory of Globalization*, Jonathan is author of the best-selling novels *Everything Is Illuminated* and *Extremely Loud and Incredibly Close*, and Joshua is, it may come as no surprise, an experiential journalist and the author of *Moonwalking with Einstein: The Art and Science of Remembering Everything*. Safran Foer, who is now the Director of the Sixth & I Historic Synagogue, a major cultural and religious center in downtown Washington, has a way with words, too. In fact, she can sum up her entire parenting—and life—philosophy in only three: "Trust your instincts."

Christine Samuel

It's ironic that Christine Samuel hails from Quitman, Mississippi, given the fact that from the day she was born, June 2, 1952, she's never quit anything—or given up on anybody. Her childhood wasn't easy, either, since after her parents divorced, she was raised solely by her mother, a maid. As an adult, she graduated from college, moved to Lauderdale Lakes, Florida, married, and gave birth to two children, a daughter, Barika, in 1976, and a son, Asante, in 1981. By the time her son reached kindergarten, she had divorced and was raising her children on her own. Though Samuel worked in the city hall in various jobs, from grant writer to legislative coordinator, a career she kept for thirty years, she still struggled to provide for her family. "She would let me and Asante eat before she ate, because it got really rough," recalls Barika, adding that about every six months they had to move after falling behind on rent. Despite the hard times, Samuel noticed early on that her son had taken a liking to football, and from the day she signed him up in the local league, when he was five, she never missed a single one of his games. Later, Asante remembers her helping him train. "My mom would be out with me at ten o'clock at night timing me in the forty in the dark," he says. By the time her son was in high school, Samuel, despite her dire financial straits, had also taken in two of his teammates, including Benny Sapp, whose father was fatally shot when Sapp was only three. "We didn't have much," she says, "but we always had love." With her support, both Asante and Sapp graduated from college and were drafted by the NFL. Asante joined the New England Patriots, where he won two Super Bowl Championships. He now plays cornerback for the Philadelphia Eagles, and he leads the NFL with thirty-seven interceptions since 2006. As a tribute to his mother, he founded Bring It Home Single Moms, a charity which provides affordable homes to low-income single mothers. Samuel's advice to those women whom her son is helping, and all new moms: "Stay close to your kids. No matter how difficult life can get, they are the greatest presents in the world."

Sunchita Tyson

Sunchita Maria Feliciano Tyson, "Toni" to her friends, was born on November 22, 1928, in New York City, the youngest of five children, to parents who had only recently migrated north from Puerto Rico. When she was three, her mother passed away, and she and her siblings were parceled out among various family members. Tyson was raised by her two beloved aunts. At twenty-four, she married Cyril DeGrasse Tyson, a sociologist, and over the next six years, gave birth to three children. Her oldest, Stephen, is a two-time Fulbright award–winning artist and college professor. Her youngest, Lynn, works in investor relations. Her middle child, Neil DeGrasse Tyson, is a world-renowned astrophysicist, director of the Hayden Planetarium in New York City, host of *Cosmos: A Space-Time Odyssey*, and author of multiple books, including his latest, *Space Chronicles: Facing the Ultimate Frontier*. "I never told my children they were brilliant. I just said do what you have to do," says Tyson, adding, "I couldn't deal with three egos. Ay yi yi." She used the city as a learning lab, taking her children to the museums and parks as often as she could, and they played at home, too. "We'd sing songs and tell stories and have the children play out the roles. I remember Neil stalking through the living room as the wolf in 'Peter and the Wolf.'" At dinner, she also encouraged her kids to give speeches about their day. "They'd introduce themselves. 'My name is Lynn Tyson. I'm in the third grade.' Then, they'd say something about their day, and thank you, and we'd all clap! I think that gave them great confidence." The most challenging part of parenting, she says, was raising her children, who all had "afros so big they'd have to go sideways through the door," during the civil rights movement of the sixties. "Integration was a big issue at the time, and I was constantly on guard to protect them from racism," says Tyson, who later became a gerontologist for the Department of Health and Human Services. "I had to make sure that when they looked at TV and saw these students being hosed, they realized that not everyone is like that. I spent a lot of time teaching them to love, not to hate." When she looks at her children and their accomplishments today, as well as her six grandchildren, she knows she succeeded. "I don't use the word 'proud,'" she says. "I feel blessed. I feel thankful, but pride does not enter."

1

Expecting

. . .

*Not only are you creating someone new,
but you are also becoming someone new.
Embrace the change.*

Spread Joy

. . .

"My brother was an ob-gyn, and when I told him I thought I was pregnant again, he said, 'Come to my office on Sunday for a sonogram, and bring the boys.' Jonathan was five and Frank was eight, and they were watching the sonogram and my brother goes, 'Yep, you're pregnant.' My husband was out of town, so we all sat down and had a little conversation about how we weren't going to tell anybody until Daddy came home. Well, we walked out of my brother's office and Jonathan stopped the first stranger he saw on the street and said, 'We're having a baby!' So we had the conversation again that we weren't going to tell anybody until Daddy got home. And the next day, he went to nursery school and said, 'We may *be having a baby.'"*

—ESTHER SAFRAN FOER

HOW TO BREAK THE NEWS

Step 1: Be certain. Home pregnancy tests are quick and cheap, but they can give you a false negative if you take them too early, drink too much water beforehand, or fail to follow the instructions to the letter. (False positives, though rare, are also possible, especially if you're taking fertility medication.) The only way to know for sure that you have a bun in the oven is by seeing your doctor and getting a blood test. Once you get those results, feel free to pop the champagne—the non-alcoholic kind, of course.

Step 2: Hug your better half. If he (or she) isn't standing ear-to-ear with you when the doctor calls with the results, then share the happy news as soon as you're ready. Some women need a minute (or hour, day, week, or even longer) to let it settle in before being able to even mouth the words, "I'm pregnant." Do what feels right to you. Just have some tissues ready when you do tell. There may be some tears, uh, hopefully the happy kind.

Step 3: Notify your inner circle. After you and your sweetie have had time to celebrate the news privately, you may want to tell your closest peeps, including your parents, siblings, or best friends. Here's the thing, though: Up to 20 percent of pregnancies result in a miscarriage, and if that's in your stars, it'll usually happen between the first and thirteenth week. So if you're bursting to share the news now and you're sure that you'll feel comfortable also sharing bad news if it comes to that, then go for it.

Step 4: Tell your boss, before your walk turns into a waddle, your belly turns into a bump, and any gossip travels to the corner office. If she finds out through someone else or because she catches you knitting some baby booties during your downtime, she may feel insulted. So, once you enter your second trimester, set a meeting for the two of you to talk, and in the meantime research your company's policy on maternity leave. When the big day arrives, go in with a smile—after all, it *is* good news you're sharing—and be prepared to offer ideas on how to cover your job while you're away.

Step 5: Tell the world. Once you're squared away with your partner, closest friends and family, and your workplace, you're free to share your good fortune with anyone you'd like, even those random high school people you friended on Facebook. If you don't take it upon yourself to do so now, your belly will do all the talking for you shortly. You'll be surprised by how many strangers will approach you on the street with a "Congratulations! Boy or girl?" Revel in the attention. Never in your life will you get so much love from so many people.

More Timeless Tips

- Get creative with your announcement, if you have the energy. Send your mom a "World's Best Grandmother" mug or text your sis a photo of your sonogram.

- If you work a dangerous job, consult your doctor for advice on when to tell your boss. You'll probably have to do it much sooner. Same goes if you have terrible morning sickness. If you're green and running to the bathroom all day, your boss is going to suspect something, and she may even be able to help you through it by working out a flexible schedule.

- Tell older children only after you've passed the thirteen-week mark to avoid any confusion or disappointment, if things don't go as planned. After that point, the younger the child, the longer you have to share the news. When you do let him know that he'll soon be a big brother, alleviate any worries that he'll be less loved by making him feel special. Give him your time and full attention and be prepared to answer any questions he may have.

Eat for Two

• • •

"I had intense cravings for tangelos. I'd eat four or five a day. Oh, and schnitzel! I remember it so clearly: I was being monitored in the hospital. It was a Sunday night, and all I wanted was a schnitzel. So my husband brought me one at 9:30 P.M. and I ate the entire thing. And then the doctor came in and told me not to have anything to eat or drink. She had to deliver my babies right away. I was about to have major surgery, and I'd just eaten an entire schnitzel. I was like, 'You know I just ate a giant schnitzel, right?' She said, 'I did see that.' My kids were born at 11 P.M."

—ERINN McGURN

HOW TO EAT WELL DURING PREGNANCY

Step 1: Quit your diet. It's hardly the time to worry over the size of your thighs. After all, you are growing an entire other human being inside of you! Your body—and your baby—need all the energy they can get. In fact, you'll need to eat roughly three hundred *extra* calories a day to help the baby flourish. Don't skimp.

Step 2: Make good choices (at least most of the time). This may be a no-brainer, but it's worth saying anyway. When you get hungry, try to choose healthier, nutrient-dense foods: fruits and vegetables, especially leafy greens; whole grains, like whole wheat bread and brown rice; lean protein, like chicken and beans; low-fat dairy, like skim milk and yogurt; and healthy fats, like avocado and olive oil.

Step 3: Avoid the no-nos. There's a bunch of stuff you shouldn't eat, so commit this list to memory: mercury-laden fish, like shark, swordfish, king mackerel, or tilefish (it could harm fetal development); soft cheeses, like Brie, Feta, and blue cheese; undercooked or raw meat, poultry, or shellfish; smoked seafood; and prepared meat like hot dogs or lunch meat, unless they're steaming hot (all could carry a bacteria called listeria, which could cause miscarriage or stillbirth); raw eggs (salmonella); and artificial sweeteners.

Step 4: Indulge (at least some of the time). You may have all sorts of intense cravings (and for food that you'd never normally eat), and you should definitely assuage them when you must. That is, after all, one of the biggest perks of pregnancy, and when else would your sweetie offer to go find a gyro and a chocolate shake for you at 11:45 P.M.? Plus, your body may be telling you it needs some key nutrients, or, you know, you could just be tired and hungry. Either way, enjoy it!

More Timeless Tips

- Eat often. Rather than eating three square meals a day, go for five or six littler ones. Frequent dining will not only help keep your blood sugar levels even, and therefore your energy up, but it'll also help you head off heartburn before it starts.

- Take a prenatal vitamin every day, if you're pregnant, trying to get pregnant, or breast-feeding. It'll help you reach your daily requirements of six hundred micrograms of folic acid (to help prevent birth defects); twenty-seven milligrams minimum of iron (to help prevent anemia); and one thousand milligrams of calcium (to help strengthen the baby's bones, heart, and nervous system; if you have too little calcium, your body steals it from your bones on behalf of the baby).

- Keep your caffeine intake to under two hundred milligrams a day. A twelve-ounce cup of coffee is fine, but any more may increase your risk of miscarriage. Too much caffeine has also been associated with preterm birth and low birth weight.

- Lay off the booze. It's up to you and your doctor to decide if a rare glass of wine is all right, but both the American College of Obstetrics and the American Academy of Pediatrics say no amount of alcohol is safe. Consumption has been linked to birth defects, mental retardation, miscarriage, low birth weight, and stillbirth.

- Even though you *can* eat so much, you may find it hard not to fixate on all the things you can't have. If you find yourself obsessing over a rare steak slathered in blue cheese and a glass of Cabernet, try to imagine just how great it'll taste in nine months. In the meantime, see page 214 for advice on finding a babysitter.

- Drink lots and lots of water. Hydration is key.

- Wash all your fruits and veggies before eating them.

Settle Down

• • •

"I remember being in a restaurant with my husband and I was nine months pregnant. All of a sudden, I just started bawling. He said, 'What's wrong?' I said, 'I have no idea!' So I went to the bathroom, wiped my eyes, came back—and it happened again! I said, 'I'm sure people think you said something terrible to me. I can't get this under control. We've got to go home!' And we did."

—ROSEMARY GIUNTA

HOW TO MANAGE YOUR MOODS

Step 1: See 'em coming. You may suddenly burst into tears at any time during your pregnancy over the littlest things, like, oh, you forgot to pick up butter at the grocery store, or you can't decide on which diaper bag you like best, *30 Rock* is a rerun tonight, or you know your totally devoted partner doesn't love you, doesn't think you're pretty, and may take off at any second. Blame your hormones, your fatigue, and the fact that a major (and somewhat stressful) life change is on the horizon. Then cut yourself some slack. You're not crazy. You're just pregnant. Crazy pregnant!

Step 2: Snooze it off. Take a nap, whenever you can. And set your DVR for your late-night shows, so you can go to bed early. You may feel especially tired during the first three months. Sometimes a good rest is all you need to reset.

Step 3: Eat well and often. When your blood sugar spikes and plummets, so does your mood. Stay even by noshing every few hours, preferably on something with a little protein, and steering clear (well, as clear as you can) of junk food binges.

Step 4: Be physical, if you can swing it. Take a walk, swim, or go to a prenatal yoga class. Exercise releases feel-good endorphins, which will help boost your mood.

Step 5: Ask for a hug. Sometimes that's what you need most.

More Timeless Tips

- If you're depressed for more than a couple of weeks, talk to your doc. She'll be able to help you feel better.

- Trust the people around you. Your partner, friends, and family are there to support you, so open up to them if you need to.

- Buy some good tissues.

- You're probably gaining weight faster than you did in your first semester of college. But know this: Though the size and shape of your body will change, you will always be beautiful, and one day you'll look back with fondness on these days you spent with your little one growing inside of you.

Rest Easy

. . .

"Because I was having twins, I was quite large and had a hard time sleeping. So I got a giant U-shaped pillow, which was a life changer. I could just roll from side to side without having to reposition nineteen pillows. I kept that pillow until my kids were four months old. Finally, my husband said, 'You've got to get rid of that thing!'"

—ERINN McGURN

HOW TO GET A GOOD NIGHT'S SLEEP

Step 1: Chill out. There's no sense in getting all riled up by watching the late night news, paying bills, or reading about the melting polar ice caps right before bed. The world can wait for you, so tell Brian Williams you'll catch up with him in a few months, and rent a season of *Downton Abbey* instead. (Seriously, it's really good.) Or take a warm bath, meditate, or read something wonderfully light.

Step 2: Climb into bed. Even if you don't feel like moving right now, it's better than the couch. Go on. You'll be happy you did.

Step 3: Roll onto your left side and bend your knees. Facing in this direction optimizes blood flow to your babe, though if you need a change, lying on your right side is also safe.

Step 4: Position your pillows. Place one between your knees, one beneath your belly, and one behind your back. Your sweetie may feel displaced by your new feather-filled friends, so don't forget to peek overtop your puff to say, "I love you," before you nod off.

Step 5: Have sweet dreams.

More Timeless Tips

- Never sleep on your back while pregnant, especially during the second and third trimesters. The added weight of the baby could smush your vena cava, a vein which carries the blood from your legs and feet back to your heart. Sleeping belly-down is also not an option, unless, of course, you enjoy sleeping on basketballs (or things that feel like basketballs). That said, your body is designed to feel most comfortable in the safest positions, so don't lie awake worrying about it, or you'll never get any sleep.

- If you wake up on your back or belly, don't fret. Simply roll back onto your side and try to drift off again.

- To help prevent heartburn, don't eat right before bed, steer clear of spicy or acidic foods (especially—just sayin'—Taco Bell Meximelts) and prop yourself up with yet another pillow.

- Lower your thermostat to between sixty and sixty-eight degrees. Sleeping in slightly chilly temps helps induce shut-eye.

Keep It Down
...

"Oh yeah, I had morning sickness. I know it feels like crap, but you just deal with it. What else are you going to do? There's no magic trick that's going to make it all go away. I drank ginger ale and ate saltines. Just know that when you have that baby, it's all worth it."

—CLAIRE BRIED

HOW TO SURVIVE MORNING SICKNESS

Step 1: Count your blessings, not your pukings. While that constant nausea, which, by the way, often lasts through the morning and into the afternoon and evening, is not at all fun, to say the least, it usually also means that your hormones are raging and your pregnancy is progressing as it should. So that's good, right? (Conversely, the absence of morning sickness doesn't mean trouble—it just means you're lucky.)

Step 2: Repeat this phrase: "This won't last forever. This won't last forever. This won't last forever." Morning sickness often dissipates after the first trimester, so even though you feel like you'll never eat or enjoy food again, you will. You just have to wait it out.

Step 3: Eat crackers in bed, especially since this may be the only time you can get away with it. Sometimes a few saltines before you rise and shine will help settle a queasy stomach. It gives the acid something to work on other than the lining of your tummy.

Step 4: Stick with boring food, and have it often. Spicy, greasy, or rich dishes and large-portion sizes may obviously exacerbate your nausea, so stick with smaller, plainer meals with plenty of complex carbs and protein, like chicken and rice or even just a baked potato with cheese. Basically, if you can get it down—and keep it down—and it has even a few nutrients in it, then yay, you!

Step 5: Stay hydrated. Drink what you can, especially if you're tossing your cookies multiple times a day. If you can't handle water, try sucking on popsicles.

Step 6: Meet your new best friend: ginger. This magical root has the power to ease your quease, thanks to the volatile oils and phenol compounds it contains. So drink ginger ale (the kind made with real ginger), eat ginger snaps, suck on ginger candy, sip ginger tea. Heck, even cut a slice of fresh ginger, wave it under your nose, and then wave good-bye to your upset tummy.

More Timeless Tips

- Get some fresh air. Your nose is more sensitive than ever right now, and sometimes the smell of cooking from your very own kitchen is enough to make you want to vomit. (No offense to your sweetie.) When that happens, try taking a walk outside.

- Wear motion sickness bands. These sweatbands come with a little plastic button on the inside, which depresses an acupressure point on the inside of your wrist. They may help you feel better, or at least momentarily distract you from your tummy woes.

• If you're up for it, acupuncture may also help soothe your stomach.

Feather Your Nest

...

"There's an old Jewish superstition to not finish the room before the baby arrives. So I painted a mural on the nursery wall, and I sewed curtains—the first and last I've ever made. And we picked out a crib, but we didn't have it delivered. Then Frank came two weeks early! So he slept in a drawer."

—ESTHER SAFRAN FOER

HOW TO ASSEMBLE A NURSERY

Step 1: Chill. Of course, you want everything in your baby's little nest to be just perfect, but if you stress over every single teensy decision you make, you'll drive yourself bonkers. After all, whichever shade of white paint you ultimately choose—Lamb or Magnolia, Heavy Cream or Picket Fence—won't matter whatsoever once your little one arrives. And understand that at some point, poop *is* going to hit that wall, so there's no need to be so precious about it.

Step 2: Find your vision. You don't necessarily have to pick a theme, like Winnie-the-Pooh or ice cream cones, but if you'd like one, that's swell. Instead, start thinking about colors and the overall style. Do you want your nursery to look modern or vintage, playful or calming? Try flipping through some home magazines or do a quick Google search. Rip out or bookmark pictures of rooms you love, and then whittle them down until you settle on your favorite.

Step 3: Clear the room. If you don't already have a dedicated vacant room for the nursery, you'll have to make one. Take a weekend or two to empty out your old office, guest room, gym, art studio, whatever. Move your furniture elsewhere (or put it in storage), empty the closets, and then give the entire space a thorough cleaning.

Step 4: Paint. Once you've chosen the color, leave the task of slapping it on the walls to your honey or a pro. Then vacate the area until it dries, because the chemicals in paint may increase your risk of miscarriage or birth defects. If you haven't figured this out already, this is the perfect excuse to plan a weekend away with the girls.

Step 5: Choose your furniture. You'll need:

• A crib. As of June 2011, every new crib on the market must meet the federal standards of the Consumer Product Safety Commission (www.cpsc.gov), so you can rest easy and just pick whichever one you like, knowing it'll be safe. Make sure you measure your space before heading to the store, though. What looks reasonably sized in a retail display may look giant in your home. If you're inheriting a crib, just make sure it's less than ten years old—any older and you're pushing it—and it meets the CPSC's essential safety requirements. You can find them here: www.cpsc.gov.

- A changing table. Go for one with a removable top, so you can use it as a dresser once your baby ages out of diapers.

You might also like:

- A rocking chair or glider. You'll spend plenty of late nights rocking your baby to sleep, and if you don't have to go very far (in the dark), your not-stubbed toes will thank you. Choose one with a high enough back to support your sleepy ol' head and arms that'll help you support your baby during feedings.

- A bookshelf. Where else are you going to keep your tattered, drool-stained copies of *Goodnight Moon*, *Pat the Bunny*, and *The Poky Little Puppy*? Just be sure the shelf is screwed into the wall, so little ones can't pull it down.

Step 6: Choose your accessories: a funky light fixture, a neat lamp, a cool mirror, custom prints from Etsy, old photos, wall decals, a sweet area rug, colorful curtains—whatever floats your boat. Have fun with color and shapes, but remember that anything you hang on the walls, especially within Baby's reach, should be fully secured. Also, your baby will be stimulated by almost anything at first, so sometimes less is more.

Step 7: Stock it. Once you've got all the major pieces in place, it's time to fill in the blanks. You'll need:

- A crib mattress. It should be firm and fit in the crib without gaps. If you can fit more than two fingers between the mattress and the crib slats, it's too small.

- A mattress pad. Get a waterproof one (or two), in case you encounter a leaky diaper or some major spit-up.

- Crib sheets. You'll need a few in case one gets wet and you haven't had a chance to launder the other.

- Blankets. Some warm fuzzies will be nice to have on hand to lay him down on or wrap him up in while you're holding him. Just remember, never put blankets in the crib with your baby; doing so increases the risk of SIDS.

- A changing pad and cover. You'll set this tiny half-mooned mattress on your changing table to help keep your baby comfy when you're wiping him down. A soft cover will make it more pleasurable for you both.

- A diaper pail. There are plenty of high-tech ones on the market, but you can also just use a regular old trash can. Just make sure that it has a lid and you're prepared to empty it daily, or things can get majorly stink-o-rama.

- Diapers and wipes. You may be tempted to buy a hefty supply, but you won't know how big your baby will be or how fast he'll grow until he arrives, so just make your best guess and get a smaller supply to start.

- A monitor. Video monitors are nice, since they allow you to not only hear your baby, but also see him, even in the dark.

- Burp cloths. Get enough so you can stash them in a few rooms. You never know when you'll need one.

- Clothes. Naked babies are scrumptious, but you'll want to dress yours to keep him happy and warm. Steer clear of separates for now (pants are a pain to take off during diaper changes) and invest in cotton onesies—long-sleeved or short-sleeved, with feeties or legless, snaps or zipper, depending on the weather and your preferences.

- A night-light. Not a floodlight, even though you may be tempted. You don't want to disturb your baby's slumber. Every wink for him (and you) is precious.

- A hamper. Keep his dirties separate from yours, because (a) some of his will probably have poop on them (and hopefully yours don't) and (b) you'll probably use gentler detergent on his clothes.

- Playthings. If you have no toys or books, everyone will be bored.

More Timeless Tips

- If you're tight on space, choose a crib with a drawer below, so you can stow extra sheets, towels, and blankets there.

- If you don't have a ceiling fan in the nursery, buy an oscillating fan and keep it running when the baby sleeps. A recent study shows it'll reduce his risk of SIDS by 72 percent.

- Check the batteries of your smoke detectors and carbon monoxide alarms before you bring the baby home. Install one in or near the nursery, if you haven't already. Also, set your water heater to 120 degrees and make sure you have a fire extinguisher on every floor of your house.

- Don't be a sucker. You can spend a fortune on baby gear, but you don't have to. If you like the looks of that $2,000 crib, look for a similar but cheaper alternative. Your baby will be just as safe, and he'll thank you when it comes time to pay for college.

Bestow Greatness

• • •

"We named Sal after his grandfather, but when we told his grandfather that, he said, 'I don't want you to. I was in the navy and they were mean to me because of my name.' I said, 'Well it looked like you handled it pretty well.' By second grade, kids started calling Sal 'Sally.' But by sixth grade, he came home and said, 'Mom, I'm really liking my name again.' When I asked him why, he said, 'When girls say it, it just sounds different.'"

—ROSEMARY GIUNTA

HOW TO CHOOSE A NAME

Step 1: Do your research. If you don't already have your heart set on a name, start looking around for possible options. A quick search online or a flip through one of the bazillion baby name books might spark inspiration, but don't forget the old-school tactics, either. Take a look at your family tree and see if any names (first *or* last) resonate with you, and also consider the heroes you may have, past and present.

Step 2: Make a list. As soon as you come across a name you like, write it down. Seeing all the candidates side by side will help you whittle your possibilities.

Step 3: Do due diligence. Once you've got a few keepers, run the following tests:

Say it three times fast: It'll help you see if the first and middle names sound good with your last name. (As a general rule of thumb, you can choose a longer first name if your last name is short and vice versa.) Also remember, your child will have to sign this name over and over throughout her life, so don't make it too laboriously long.

Check the initials: Anne Suzanne Smith might sound good to you, but in thirty years, do you really want your daughter to carry around an embroidered L.L.Bean tote that says ASS on the side?

Test the teases: Kids can be cruel, so think twice before naming your son something like Richard Harding or John Flushing.

Do the Google test: Enter your chosen name in the search bar to see if it (or anything close in sound or spelling) is shared by anyone famous or infamous. You don't want to saddle your kid with the duty of explaining, "No, I'm Justin Beeber, not Justin Bieber."

Step 4: Make your choice. Then, rejoice! You've just made one of the biggest decisions you'll ever make.

More Timeless Tips

- Steer clear of unique spellings. Jenee and Bawb may seem crazy and cool now, but you'll doom your child to a lifetime of typos.

- Once you've found your keeper, it's up to you whether you want to keep it a secret or share it with friends and family prior to the birth. If you do share, just be warned: Your audience will offer their feedback.

- If you're stressing about this decision, remember that after your baby arrives, the name you give him will be his, and soon enough, it'll be hard to imagine the possibility of him being called anything else.

Choose Well
...

*"You do what your doctor tells you, and whether he knows
what he's doing is up to the good lord."*
—BETTY HORTON

HOW TO FIND A GOOD OBSTETRICIAN

Step 1: Get references. If you already have an ob-gyn you know and love, who delivers babies, then hallelujah! You're all set. If not, ask for recommendations from your friends, coworkers, family members, and family doctor. You can also scoot around online—check with message boards of local parents' groups, the American College of Obstetrics and Gynecology (acog.org), and your insurance company.

Step 2: Make an appointment. Once you find a doctor with lots of fans (and, let's not forget, who also accepts your insurance), request a consultation. Your goal: to get a sense of her bedside manner, as well as her philosophy of practice. If she's curt, return to Step 1. Ditto, if she's condescending or dismissive. You want a doctor who listens to you and respects you and your decisions.

Step 3: Ask questions. A few biggies:

• What's your c-section rate? The national c-section
  rate is up to 34 percent, so if you're hoping to have
  a low-intervention birth, choose a doctor who bests
  that.

• Which hospital are you affiliated with? You may love the
  doctor, but if she delivers at a joint clear across town,
  consider whether you'll be able to make it there when
  you're in labor, which will no doubt happen at rush
  hour.

• Who else is in your practice? The more doctors in rotation,
  the less likely yours will be on call when you deliver. Find
  out who exactly you'll be seeing during your regular visits
  and who is on backup if your doc happens to be lying on a
  beach in the Bahamas on your due date.

• How do you feel about [insert your concern here]? Ask
  about anything that's important to you. How do you feel
  about unmedicated births? Can my mom and two sisters
  join me in the delivery room? How do you feel working
  with midwives or doulas? Can I e-mail you with any
  questions or concerns? Will you allow me to eat Ben &
  Jerry's while in labor? No question is stupid, if it's on your
  mind.

Step 4: Exhale. Once you've found a doctor you like and trust,
then you can relax, knowing that you're in good hands.

More Timeless Tips

- If you have a low-risk pregnancy or you prefer to deliver at home or in a birthing center, you may also consider using a certified nurse-midwife. Not only can she help deliver your baby, she can care for you throughout your pregnancy, prescribing medicine and ordering tests when need be.

- When you make a doctor's appointment, try to snag the first slot of the day, when wait times are generally much shorter.

Choose Well Again

• • •

"A good doctor does not talk down to you and is polite and, furthermore, answers your questions directly and never just says, 'Don't worry about that.'"

—SUNCHITA TYSON

HOW TO FIND A GOOD PEDIATRICIAN

Step 1: Get a jump-start. Do not wait until you've got a screaming baby in your hands to find a doctor for her. Instead, as soon as you tilt into your third trimester, start getting personal recommendations from all the usual suspects: your friends, family members, neighbors, and doctors. You can also visit the American Academy of Pediatrics website at healthychildren.org to find a board-certified doctor near you.

Step 2: Set up an interview. Once you find a few candidates (who, you know, also accept your insurance), take an afternoon or two to make the rounds and meet them. (Some even have new parent meet-and-greets on certain nights of the week.) You'll quickly get a sense of their bedside manner as well as how their offices are run.

Step 3: Ask questions. A few of the biggies:

- How long have you been practicing?

- What are your hours?

- Who can I call if my child gets sick after hours or on a weekend?

- Do you offer same-day sick visits?

- Which hospital are you affiliated with?

- Do you handle all appointments yourself, or will I see other doctors or nurse practitioners?

- How do you feel about vaccinations? Antibiotics?

- Can I call or e-mail with non-emergency questions?

Step 4: Make your decision. And, after you do, fill the pediatrician in on your family history and any active issues in your pregnancy, such as gestational diabetes or an irregular sonogram, so she's prepared for your first visit.

Step 5: Wait for Baby. After you choose your pediatrician, there's nothing more to do until you actually give birth. Once your bundle of joy arrives, call your doctor (if you've delivered at a hospital she's not affiliated with and she's not already seen you) and make your first appointment. The American Academy of Pediatrics recommends that you see your pediatrician two to three days after a normal, uncomplicated delivery. You may even see her a second time within that first week home for another weigh-in and checkup.

More Timeless Tips

• Always trust your gut, unless of course, your gut is telling you to drink *another* milkshake, in which case, read the advice starting on page 7 (how to eat well during pregnancy). Then, have the milkshake, if you must, and then, finally, choose your doctor.

Round Up

· · ·

"Accept the fear you feel, but know that it'll go away. It won't feel so scary all the time. And don't be embarrassed to ask questions. The more you do, the better you'll feel. It helps take away the fear. There are no stupid questions for a brand-new or expecting mom."

—ROSEMARY GIUNTA

HOW TO FIND SUPPORT

Step 1: Share the news. It's tough to get encouragement from others if no one has any idea what's going on with you, so start spilling the beans. You'll find other moms are especially sympathetic to anything you may be going through—the worry, the morning sickness, the swollen ankles—because they've been there, too.

Step 2: Ask for help when you need it. You've probably never been more tired/nauseated/anxious ever in your life, which means you've probably never felt quite so vulnerable. Don't be afraid to enlist your friends or family members to help you with the little things, like grocery shopping, a ride to the doctor's office, even an occasional ice cream run. Most will be only too happy to do so.

Step 3: Expand your circle. Nobody is more in tune to what you're experiencing than other expectant moms, so put yourself in situations where you can meet and talk with them. Take a pre-natal yoga class, enroll in a childbirth education class with your sweetie, log on to message boards online. It's important to remember that you are never alone.

More Timeless Tips

- You'll probably begin to find that your friends who already have kids haven't talked with you about things like, say, indigestion or perineum massage, because they didn't want to be *that* kind of mom. But here's the secret: They're actually dying to. Take advantage of their knowledge, experience, and friendship.

Stock Up

· · ·

*"I made maximum use of our freezer. I froze everything in sight!
I could go days without having to shop. My specialty
was Spanish rice and beans."*

—Sunchita Tyson

How to Fill Your Freezer for Later

Step 1: Harness your energy. During your second trimester
and also the tail end of your third, you'll likely experience sudden
jolts of much-needed nesting energy. Use those spurts to plan for
your culinary future, since you'll be short on sleep once the baby
arrives.

Step 2: Embrace the casserole. You won't have time to cook, or
grocery shop, once your baby arrives, and Chinese takeout only
satisfies for so long. So call your mom, or browse through old cook-
books or online, for recipes that you can make ahead and freeze.

Look for ones heavy on the protein (chicken, beef, etc.), because they'll help you stay awake at least long enough to eat your next bite.

Step 3: Cook like you've never cooked before, and put everything you make in your freezer, labeled with the contents and the date you made it. It may feel like hard work now, but you'll be so happy you did it.

More Timeless Tips

- When planning your menu, steer clear of especially gassy or spicy foods, if you plan on breast-feeding, or you may wind up with a fussy baby. Swap the three-alarm beef chili for turkey and mashed potatoes, and the cabbage soup for carrot soup.

- Not enough pans? Invest in a few disposable aluminum ones.

- Consider packaging your food into smaller servings, so you don't have to eat an entire tray of chicken lasagna at back-to-back meals. Everything will taste better if you can muster a little variety by rotating your meals throughout the week.

Roll Out

• • •

"Bring only the necessary things. You're probably going to be in a hospital gown and glad of it. You really need so little."
—RUTH ALSOP

HOW TO PACK YOUR HOSPITAL BAG

Step 1: Gather your clothes. You'll need:

- Sleeping attire: If you're not into the whole hospital gown look, bring something loose and comfy to sleep (and hang out and get pictures taken) in. Just be sure whatever you choose offers easy access to your breasts if you plan on nursing.

- Granny pants: Go for undies so baggy, they'd embarrass you under any other circumstance. (The hospital will give you undies, too, but they're flimsy and weird.) Whichever pair you choose, you'll be stuffing giant maxi pads in them anyway.

- A few nursing bras

- Socks

- Slippers

- A going-home outfit for you: You can't go wrong with sweats or yoga pants and a comfy shirt, with sneakers.

Don't pack your pre-pregnancy clothes, either. You'll still look kinda pregnant even after your delivery.

Step 2: Round up your toiletries, including:

• Your toothbrush and toothpaste

• A comb and brush, plus whatever else you need (hair ties, a hairdryer, etc.)

• Glasses, contact lens case and solution

• Makeup

• Maxi pads: The hospital will provide some ginormous old-school ones, but you might be more comfy in others.

• Travel-size shampoo, conditioner, soap, and lotion: Hospitals aren't exactly known for their selection of Molton Brown products.

Step 3: Bring a few things for your baby, including:

• A going-home outfit: Keep her comfort in mind, before you pick up a frilly dress. Also, make sure it's weather appropriate.

• A blanket

• A few diapers and wipes: The hospital will give you some, but you should get into the habit of bringing these wherever you go.

Step 4: Pack your labor supplies, including:

- Your birth plan, if you have one (See "How to Get What You Need at the Hospital" for tips on making one on page 64.)

- A birthing ball: Sitting, rocking, and leaning on an exercise ball can help you through your labor.

- A massager: Two tennis balls in a knotted tube sock work well.

- A music player: Ask if your hospital offers iPod docks, and then make a playlist to listen to during labor. Disco ball optional.

- Snacks: If your doctor gives you the OK to eat during labor, pack a few healthy bites. Think trail mix and energy bars, not Cheetos and licorice.

- A picture of your loves: Think your other children, your puppy, your favorite beach, any image that makes you feel strong and happy.

Step 5: Pack the essentials, including:

- Your wallet with ID and insurance card

- Your phone

- A camera

- Your keys

- A car seat: You won't be allowed to leave the hospital with your baby without one. Make sure the base is already properly installed in your car. At nhtsa.gov find a certified technician near you to check it for free.

More Timeless Tips

• If you can swing it, bring a treat for your labor and delivery nurses. A happy, well-appreciated staff will treat you much better than a cranky, hungry one, so keep a box of chocolates or a batch of cookies at the ready. Plus, it's nice to spend the day before delivery, or even early labor, making chocolate chip cookies. No time? No worries. The doctors and nurses who deliver babies do it because they love babies (yes, even more than cookies).

• Don't overdo it. You want to take one bag, which means you won't need ten pairs of wool socks.

Cherish

· · ·

"Becoming parents shifts your dynamic as a couple so if you don't feel solid and supported, being a new parent can be isolating. So build your strength: Talk about the changes that are coming, because they are coming. It's a good time to bolster your relationship. We always said, 'We made these two little people together. They're ours!'"

—Erinn McGurn

HOW TO MAKE THE MOST OF YOUR LAST MONTHS AS A COUPLE

Step 1: Plan dates. Right now, you and your sweetie are able to devote 100 percent of your attention to each other. You're able to spontaneously catch a movie. You can enjoy a leisurely meal in a fancy restaurant. You can have an uninterrupted conversation about anything you'd like. All of those things will become a lot more difficult once your baby arrives, so relish the one-on-one time you have together now. Get dressed up, gaze into each other's eyes, hold hands, talk about something other than which crib to buy, and, not to sound hokey, but remember that your love for each other is the foundation upon which you'll build your family. Nurture it. Aww!

Step 2: Get it on. Hopefully, your raging hormones have turned you into a sex machine, but even if they haven't, do whatever you need to do to get in the mood. Turn the lights low, light a candle, put on the Barry White. Not only will you not be allowed to do It for at least six weeks post-delivery, but you may not really want to even after that, when you're sleep-deprived and you've got a sleeping (and frequently *not* sleeping) baby in the next room. Take the time to connect now.

Step 3: Take walks. Not only will they be your last strolls sans stroller, but they're also a great way to stay healthy and, in those last few weeks of your pregnancy, even encourage labor. Plus, you'll find that it's lovely walking hand in hand with your sweetie, while passersby smile at you and your great belly.

Step 4: Chill together. When you get into the home stretch, you'll probably not feel like doing much of anything but lounging on the couch. Make it a pairs activity by cuddling up together and renting or downloading a season's worth of juicy, fun TV, like *The Wire*, *Sons of Anarchy*, *The Sopranos*, *Six Feet Under*, or *Battlestar Galactica*.

More Timeless Tips

- Your sweetie might not know exactly how to "be there" for you or be close to you during this time, particularly if your pre-pregnancy time together always started with a bottle of champagne and ended with your panties on the chandelier. So just communicate with him (or her), and chances are your partner will do whatever he (or she) can to make you happy.

2

Delivering

. . .

You are strong enough. Your body knows what to do.
And besides, this is the sweetest pain you will ever feel.

Count Down

• • •

"My water only broke with one of my kids. So when you'd get that pain, then you'd time it. They're six minutes apart, then five minutes, and then you think, Well pretty soon we've got to get to the hospital. We didn't take classes or anything. I had no idea what to expect, so I was a little scared. But it's something you learn."

—MARY HUFF

HOW TO RECOGNIZE SIGNS OF LABOR

Step 1: Check your house. Have you just reorganized every drawer, cupboard, and closet in the joint? Have you decided now might be a good time to reupholster your couch yourself? Do you have a sudden urge to scrub your bathroom tiles with a toothbrush, you know, for fun? If so, your delivery may be imminent. While pregnancy brings out your nesting instincts, they usually kick into overdrive shortly before labor.

Step 2: Check your profile. Stand in front of a mirror and eyeball your baby bump. If it looks considerably lower than you remember, you could go into labor within a few weeks—or hours. Your baby has dropped, or snuggled into your pelvis in preparation for his grand entrance. You've got to give it to him: He knows how to create a sense of drama.

Step 3: Check your undies. Gross, but also informative. A few days (or moments) before you go into labor, you'll lose your mucus plug, which is basically the cork that's been preventing bacteria from entering the uterus all these months. It'll look like—are you ready for this?—a glob of chicken fat, and it may have a teeny bit of blood in it, due to your cervix dilating. Hey, you were warned!

Step 4: Check the floor. If you see a puddle beneath you, either your water has broken or it's raining. If it's the former, that means the amniotic sac that has held and protected your baby all these months has ruptured and the fluid is trickling, or gushing, out of you. Once your bag breaks, your baby is more susceptible to infection, so it's time to call your doctor and get this show on the road. Your contractions will probably start within hours or moments, and if they don't, your doctor will likely induce you. Many women jump ahead to step five before this one, so know that if your water doesn't break, that does not mean you're *not* in labor.

Step 5: Check your watch. When your contractions start, you'll feel some aching in your lower back and belly. That's your uterus squeezing and releasing and your cervix dilating. In real labor, your contractions will become stronger, longer, and closer together, and if you notice that they're following this pattern, then—woo hoo!—this is it! Call your doctor. If, however, your contractions don't come regularly, then chances are you're in false labor. These psych-out contractions, known as Braxton Hicks, are caused by your uterus just practicing for the big day. They'll often go away if you eat something or move around. Just keep monitoring them, because one of these days, the real thing is going to come, and a whole other human being is going to emerge from your body. Mind-blowing!

More Timeless Tips

• To time your contractions, check your watch when one starts and again when the next one starts. There are also smart-phone apps that do this for you, but unless your sweetie is a tech genius, go old-school on it. When the time comes, you'll be so excited that even a watch will suddenly seem complex. Make it easy on yourself and keep it simple.

• When you do go into labor, take a few deep breaths, try to stay calm, and, if you can, grab something bland to eat. Make that very bland. Your delivery will go much more smoothly if your body has fuel.

• If you're not sure whether you're in labor or not, don't guess, and don't be shy either. Just call your doctor, even if it's the middle of the night. That's what he's there for.

Drive Well

...

"My husband drove me to the hospital. I remember he was kind to another driver and I didn't want him to be. I said, 'Cut him off and get me to the hospital!' He wasn't driving fast enough. Even so, we made it in time. We were hours *early!"*

—RUTH ALSOP

HOW TO MAKE IT TO THE HOSPITAL IN TIME

Step 1: Get a driver. No, you don't need a fancy chauffeur or limousine, just someone who can remain cool-headed enough to navigate the roads while you're doing what you're going to be do-ing: breathing, eating, yelling, whatever. If your spouse isn't up to the task or would rather be in the backseat holding your hand, enlist a friend and put her on speed dial.

Step 2: Map your route. You won't have the time or patience to stop and ask for directions, so it's best to know where you're going in advance. Also, have a few backup routes in mind, in case there's traffic, construction, or a parade in town.

Step 3: Practice the drive. Take the trip at different times of day: during the day, during rush hour, and at night. That way, you'll know how much time you'll need to get there on The Big Day.

Step 4: Stay calm. The movies may not have you believe this, but very few women actually give birth in the backseat of a car. In fact, average first labor lasts about twenty-four hours, so there's no need to drive like a maniac. You'll most likely have plenty of time to get to the hospital. Tell your driver to obey all traffic laws, including speed limits and red lights.

Step 5: Know where to park. The last thing you want to do when you arrive at the hospital is to troll around, looking for a parking spot. So find out in advance if the hospital has a valet service, a free parking lot, or a nearby pay lot. Plot the proper hospital entrance, too, so you know where to get close to.

More Timeless Tips

- There's no need to hop into the car at the first sign of labor. Instead, follow the 411 rule: Go when your contractions are four minutes apart, one minute long, and have been that way for one hour. If your contractions are coming so quickly that you can't remember what 411 stands for, chances are you should get to the hospital stat.

- Never, ever try to drive yourself to the hospital while you're in labor. It's just not safe for you, your baby, or any other driver on the road. If you don't have a ride to the hospital, call a car service or a cab, or go knock on your friendly neighbor's door. If you're alone and in labor, call 911.

• Always, always wear your seat belt.

Pop the Cork

· · ·

"Kristin was late, so we'd drive on these bumpy Spanish roads to try to get things going. I just wanted to get it started so badly. You? You were late, too, and had to be induced. They used Pitocin. It's instant and intense, and there's no building up. I much preferred the driving-on-bumpy-Spanish-roads method."

—CLAIRE BRIED

HOW TO INDUCE LABOR NATURALLY

Step 1: Wait. You obviously don't want to go into labor early, but if your due date has whizzed by with nothing so much as a twinge down below, then it may be time to take matters into your own hands. Consult your doctor first, of course.

Step 2: Rub your nubs. Yep. There you go. Stimulating your nipples, or better yet, having your sweetie give 'em a swirl, might trigger a release of oxytocin in your body, which is a natural labor inducer. The only catch is, you've got to do it for hours, not minutes, a day. Enjoy!

Step 3: Have sex. Hopefully, after Step 2, Step 3 will be inevitable. Lucky you, because the physical contractions of an orgasm may be just the spark you need to kick-start the contractions of childbirth. Semen, if you're getting some of that stuff, also contains prostaglandins, which can help ripen the cervix. Who knew?

Step 4: Walk. The gentle up-and-down motion of your stride may help your baby settle into your pelvis, putting pressure on your cervix and encouraging it to open.

Step 5: Get acupuncture. Studies suggest that inserting a few teeny tiny needles at special points on your body can indeed start labor, reduce the length of labor, and reduce the chances of a cesarean section. Even though acupuncture sounds painful, it's not at all. You hardly feel the needles go in, and if you do, it feels like someone just gently flicked you.

Step 6: Try acupressure. Place your fingers together, lay your pinky on your anklebone, and find the spot above it where your index finger rests. Then, press there and hold it for a minute or so. Repeat as necessary. This ancient Chinese medicine, like acupuncture, frees your body's energy (or qi) to help it work more optimally.

Step 7: Move along. Not only is this one gross *and* not necessarily supported by science, but generations of women will attest to the fact that eating spicy foods or even drinking castor oil (but only if you're beyond two centimeters dilated) will stimulate your pooper, which will, in turn, stimulate your uterus. Just be sure you're plenty hydrated and you've got good reading material in the bathroom.

More Timeless Tips

- Don't ask why it works, but many women swear that eating pineapple, eggplant parmesan, or okra can induce labor.

- Ask your doctor or midwife before trying any herbal remedies, like raspberry leaf tea, black haw, evening primrose oil, or black cohosh. Although there's not much research on the role of herbal remedies in labor induction (yet), many swear by them.

Go Natural

. . .

*"I had a natural delivery. No drugs. I was very calm.
Asante arrived like lightning, and later, when he started walking,
he took off like lightning, too."*

—Christine Samuel

HOW TO ENCOURAGE A HEALTHY DELIVERY

Step 1: Choose a doctor you trust. Since 1996, the United States has seen a 50 percent increase in cesarean sections, which means about one in three women deliver this way, despite the fact that the AAP recommends vaginal delivery in most cases. (It's generally better for the baby and the mother.) Unfortunately, some docs encourage a C-section when it's not medically necessary for reasons including liability issues, convenience, and, if they're super sketchy, even higher billing rates. So if you're hoping for a vaginal birth, hire a doctor whose cesarean rate is lower than the national average, and ask her under what conditions she'd recommend one.

Step 2: Stay nourished. Make sure your muscles, including your uterus, don't tire out on you halfway through your delivery, by giving them loads of energy when your labor starts. So, especially early on, eat whatever gives you comfort. Once you move into active labor, your doc may allow you to continue snacking. If so, pack easy-to-handle bites, like trail mix or an energy bar.

Step 3: Drink. Admit it, you were hoping this meant vodka, weren't you? Sorry to dash your hopes, but (a) you're still pregnant and (b) a drunk lady in labor would be a royal disaster. For now, just stick with water or an energy drink, like Gatorade, and have a sip after every single contraction, even if you're not thirsty. Once you move into active labor, your hospital may only allow you to eat ice chips. It's not that doctors like being mean. It's because if you do have to have an emergency C-section with general anesthesia, any food in your belly could come back up and block your airway. It's as rare as rare can be, but it's also best to be safe.

Step 4: Have good support. Your sweetie, mom, sister, or best friend may all be kick-ass labor coaches, but if you want a ringer, consider hiring a doula. Studies show that when you have a professional support person (who is not on the hospital staff) by your side throughout delivery, you'll be more likely to have a vaginal birth, a shorter labor, and a self-described positive experience.

Step 5: Postpone your epidural. Women who get an epidural during labor are 3.7 times more likely to have a C-section than those who don't, according to a study in *Obstetrics and Gynecology.* That number jumps even higher among those who get the epidural early on in labor. So, if you can, try to wait until you're dilated four or five centimeters before opting for sweet relief. Just think: A few more *minutes* of pain now may make for a few *weeks* less pain during your recovery.

More Timeless Tips

- Be sure to have plenty of straws handy for the big day. When you're in labor, it's way easier to sip from one than from a cup, especially if your partner is holding it for you.

- Remember that your *only* goal throughout your entire pregnancy is to deliver a healthy baby. How your bundle of joy arrives—vaginally or via C-section, naturally or with loads of pain medication—will make no difference in the long run, so don't worry too much on the details. Just keep the big picture in mind.

Exhale

. . .

"Breathing is just a mind game. It gives you something to focus on while your body is doing something else. I'd breathe and focus on a point, and when a contraction came and I wasn't supposed to push, that's when I did the hee-hoos. You have to believe it'll work. That's half the battle. Then you do what you have to do because you want that baby."

—Claire Bried

HOW TO BREATHE

Step 1: Forget everything you've seen in the movies. You are by no means required to say "hee-hee-hee-hoo-hoo-hoo" during every breath, unless, of course, something really funny just happened, or you're into that.

Step 2: Inhale through your nose. Take a long, slow breath in, filling your lungs as deeply as you can. Your mission: to oxygenate your blood. It'll help your body to perform at its optimum and your baby to breathe.

Step 3: Exhale through your mouth. Keep it low and slow as you visualize the pain leaving your body.

More Timeless Tips

- When you focus your mind on your breath, it can help distract you from your pain. Double down by counting to four on each inhale and exhale.

Find Focus

• • •

"I accepted the pain, because I knew it wasn't going away. If I'm going to whine at five, what am I going to do at ten? I never had the epidural for any of my kids, even though I found out you just don't go straight to heaven because you give birth without one."

—ROSEMARY GIUNTA

HOW TO COPE WITH PAIN

Step 1: Enlist gravity. When your contractions start, you by no means have to climb into bed and stay horizontal until your little peanut pops out. In fact, remaining in an upright position may actually help ease your pain and speed your labor. Stand, walk, or rock from side to side. Try leaning forward, placing your hands on your knees (or your arms around your partner's neck) for support. Or sit on a backwards chair, or kneel on the floor, draping your arms over a birthing ball.

Step 2: Use water. Ice feels great on your lower back, and nothing beats a cool washcloth on your forehead during labor. Also, a warm shower can distract you from early contractions. Save a warm bath to relieve more intense pain, the kind you feel at five centimeters and higher.

Step 3: Create an ambiance. There's nothing soothing about glaring lights and loud beeps, and when you're hurting, annoyances like these can worsen your perception of pain. So make your environment in the hospital as nice as you can: Draw the shades, dim the lights, bring a portable MP3 player and pipe in some tunes. You get no additional points for putting up with the work of those lousy interior decorators that hospitals always seem to employ.

Step 4: Ask for a massage. If you're into it, it could help distract you, ease your pain, and reduce your anxiety. (If you're not, it could make you want to slap somebody.) Your partner or support person can start with your head, hands, and feet, and then move on to your shoulders or back. Think light stroking, not deep Swedish kneading.

Step 5: Make some noise. You may be embarrassed at first, but by the time you get toward the end of your labor, you won't give two hoots about what anybody thinks of how you look or sound. So until it's time to push, don't hold anything in. Vocalizing during your contractions—moaning, cursing, counting, humming, or praying—will help you loosen your jaw, which will help loosen your pelvic floor. Just try to avoid screechy sounds, and instead keep your tones low and open. Remember, you're after a baby, not a Grammy.

Step 6: Visualize. Rather than focus on what hurts or what may go wrong, replace your worry with positive thoughts and images. Never underestimate the mind-body connection. Think (or even say), Open, open, open, and your body will do just that.

More Timeless Tips

- Pain is not a sign that your labor is going wrong. It's merely a side effect of a perfectly healthy labor. So, try not to fear or fight it. Instead, simply let it pass through you.

- Some contractions may feel like they'll never end, but they will. No contraction, even the worst of the worst, lasts more than ninety seconds. You can do anything for ninety seconds.

- After each contraction, say to yourself, "You never have to do that one again" and/or "I'm one step closer to meeting my baby."

Bear Down

...

"Because my mother had eight children, and I never heard any horror stories from her, I thought there'd be nothing to the delivery. You just go in, have the baby, and don't dwell on it. Well, I was in for a big surprise when the labor pains hit, let me tell you! It was intense. When my husband came into the room, I said, 'I am never doing this again!' I wish I would've better prepared myself mentally. And the next time, with Rachel, I was."

—ELAINE MADDOW

HOW TO PUSH

Step 1: Throw all modesty out the window. You're about to moan and groan, flash all your parts to everyone in the room, and—hate to say it—probably poop on the delivery table. Know that that's all part of the normal birthing process. Everybody does it, so try not to get suddenly shy. Release your inhibitions and you'll have a smoother birth.

Step 2: Get into position. Squatting is always good, because you'll have gravity on your side. If you're not into that, try lying back in a semi-reclined position and putting your knees up in the air. Your nurses and/or support person can help you out by holding them up for you.

Step 3: Wait for the sensation (and your doctor's instructions). Usually when it's time to push, you'll know it because there is absolutely nothing else in the world you'd rather do at that very moment. When you feel it coming on, tell your doctor, and if she gives you the thumbs-up, go for it.

Step 4: Give it your all. Tuck your chin into your chest, take a deep breath, close your eyes, and push with all of your might, engaging the same muscles you would if you were pooping. Childbirth is a beautiful, magical, wonderful thing. It just happens to feel as if you're taking the biggest, most glorious poop of your life.

More Timeless Tips

• Try keeping your upper body relaxed. Hunching your shoulders only leaches the energy you should be sending toward your bottom.

• When it's time to push, you've got two good breath options: (1) exhale with every push or (2) hold your breath, tuck your chin, and squeeze. Just do whichever comes naturally.

• Your doctor may instruct you not to push during certain contractions in order to reduce tearing. If that's the case, you'll just have to breathe through it. Look your support person in the eye and repeatedly blow out, like you're blowing out birthday candles, until the contraction ends.

Speak Up

• • •

"I wasn't that demanding. I said, 'You do your job, and I'll do mine.'"

—Sunchita Tyson

HOW TO GET WHAT YOU NEED AT THE HOSPITAL

Step 1: Get educated. A few weeks, or months, before you're due, take a tour of the labor and delivery unit. Not only will you learn about the hospital protocol, it'll be a great opportunity for you to ask questions, while you're, you know, not in the middle of having a baby.

Step 2: Make a birth plan. Keep in mind that Mother Nature is running this show, which means you may not have quite as much control over it as you'd like. To avoid being disappointed, jot down your general expectations, as opposed to your minute-by-minute plan. Some things to think about: If and when you'd like pain medication, if you'd like to move around during labor, who you'd like in the delivery room, who you'd like to cut the cord, and whether you plan on breast-feeding. Once you complete it, share it with your doctor to make sure everyone is on the same page before the big event.

Step 3: Have an advocate. If things aren't happening the way you'd like, trust your support person to represent your needs and desires to your doctors and nurses. Preferably, he or she will do this out of your earshot, so you can concentrate on what really matters: Bringing your baby into this world.

More Timeless Tips

- Be friendly. Having a baby doesn't give you permission to be a witch (with a B). There will be times when you need more ice chips, another pillow, a dimmer light, or another gown. Your nurses will respond much sooner to you if you simply use your manners. Say please and thank you. Easy.

- If things don't go exactly as you'd planned, and again chances are they won't, don't lash out at the staff. Instead, be flexible and it'll be a better experience for everyone, including your baby.

Give Love

· · ·

"I held each of you after you were born. I was surprised how little and wrinkly you were, but I thought you were each the most beautiful thing I'd ever seen."

—CLAIRE BRIED

HOW TO BOND WITH YOUR NEWBORN

Step 1: Hold her. As soon as possible after your baby is born, when she's quiet, alert, and responsive, open your gown (if you're still wearing one) and place her directly on your chest. This skin-to-skin contact is one of life's sweetest pleasures, and it's been shown to be mutually beneficial to both mother and baby. Not only will it help you feel connected, increase your milk supply, and boost your confidence, it'll also help regulate her heartbeat, breathing, and temperature. (File this under Wow: Your breasts will automatically get hotter or colder, depending on what she requires.) Furthermore, babies who've been held this way have also been shown to sleep better, cry less, and gain weight faster. Do it as long and as often as you can, and the comfort you provide each other in the first few hours and days after birth may enhance your bond for life.

Step 2: Breast-feed, if you can. When you nurse your baby, not only do you and your baby stay in close contact, but your body also releases a surge of oxytocin, a hormone that facilitates bonding and promotes milk letdown. (Incidentally, that hormone is also released when you have an orgasm, which explains all that lovey-dovey pillow talk afterward.) Studies also show that nursing mothers tend to be more responsive to their infants, touch them more often during both feedings and playtime, and spend more time gazing into their baby's eyes (and vice versa).

Step 3: Gaze in her eyes. Put your face close to hers—she can only see clearly for eight to fifteen inches—and lock peepers, while feeding her or smiling, talking or singing to her. Because she's drawn to high-contrast objects, like your eyes and mouth, she'll look back at you, and from that moment on, you'll be hers forever.

Step 4: Spend as much time together as possible. If, when your baby is born, you look at her and think, Who is this wrinkly, squirmy, noisy, messy, alien creature that I'm suddenly expected to care for around the clock? Don't worry. You are not alone. Some parents connect instantly with their pups, while other parent-child pairs require a little more time to get to know each other. If you are among the latter, simply repeat Steps 1, 2, and 3, and before you know it, you'll be bonded for life.

More Timeless Tips

- If you're doing things around the house or running errands, consider wearing your baby in a baby carrier.

- If after two weeks you still feel like you haven't bonded with your baby, or you're feeling anxious, sad, or irritable, mention it to your doctor. You may be suffering from postpartum depression, and you don't have to be. It's totally common and totally treatable, and it's nothing to be ashamed of.

3

Nourishing

. . .

You've got one more mouth to feed. Do it well.

Be a Sucker

...

"I nursed my girls, because it was just natural. I spent nine months having them, so I spent nine months nursing them, too. It was good for them."

—BETTY HORTON

HOW TO BREAST-FEED

Step 1: Settle in. Gather any supplies you may need—a pillow on your lap (to support the baby), a burp cloth, and a glass of water for yourself—and nuzzle into a calm, quiet place, where both you and your baby can focus on the task at hand.

Step 2: Position your baby. Here are a few good holds for feeding from your left breast (just switch 'em around to feed from your right side):

- The Cradle: Lay your baby across your lap, so his body is turned completely toward you and your bellies are touching. Allow his head to rest in the crook of your left arm. This one is great for pros, since you can use your free hand to hold a book, magazine, or phone.

- The Cross-Cradle: Lay your baby across your lap, turned so she's facing you. Support her head and neck with your right

hand by placing your thumb and pointer behind each ear
and the palm of your hand between her shoulder blades.
Her head should rest comfortably in the webbing of your
hand. This one is great for beginners, since you can use
your free hand to help your baby latch on.

- The Football: Lay your baby along your left side, so his
head rests just beneath your breast. Use your left forearm
(and a pillow beneath) to support his body and your left
hand to support his head. Though his head, shoulders, and
hips should be in a straight line, you may have to send his
feet upward if you're leaning back in a chair or against a
pillow. This one is especially great if you've had a C-section
and your belly is sore.

- The Side-Lying Hold: Lie down with your baby, facing
each other, with her nose even with your nipple and her legs
pulled in toward you. Use your right hand to gently guide
her to your breast. This one is great for when you're
chilling on the couch or in bed. Just make sure you're
wide-awake, though. If you fall asleep next to your baby,
you risk rolling onto her and suffocating her.

Step 3: Support your breast. Cup your hand behind your areola,
placing your thumb on one side and your fingers on the other, and
gently compress it, so your nipple stands at attention.

Step 4: Encourage your baby to open up. Bring him toward
your breast (not the other way around), aiming your nipple toward
his nose. His lower lip should brush your breast about an inch beneath your nipple, which will trigger his rooting reflex; infants will

turn and try to suck on anything that brushes their cheek or lip. Eager to eat, he'll open wide.

Step 5: Flick it in. There's no better way to describe it. Once your baby opens her mouth, flick your nipple into it, and she'll latch on. You know you've got a good latch if most of your areola (not just your nipple) is in her mouth and it doesn't hurt when she sucks. You may feel like you're jamming your entire boob into her mouth, but check out her big mouth and tiny receding chin. See? She's built to open wide for Mama. If she doesn't latch on properly and only takes the tip of your nip in her mouth, she won't get enough milk and eventually you'll get sore, cracked nipples. To correct it, slip your pinky into her mouth to break the seal and try again. It may take a few tries, especially at first, so just be patient.

Step 6: Look for swallowing. Make sure your baby is drinking (and not just using you as a pacifier) by looking for a moving jaw, ear, and temple and a bullfrog throat. Also, listen for gulps followed by soft exhales. Babies swallow about every three sucks.

Step 7: Switch breasts, and repeat until your baby pops himself off. The next time you feed him, start with the side you ended on to ensure even milk production in both breasts.

More Timeless Tips

- Watch for early hunger cues, and feed your baby as soon as you see them. She'll smack her lips, make a sucking motion with her mouth, move her head toward your breast (or any-thing else in the vicinity that could remotely feel like a breast that may or may not belong to you), kick, squirm, look around or, at long last, cry.

• If your baby nods off early on in the meal, try rousing him by stroking his cheek, blowing his hair, burping him, or even changing his diaper.

• You know your baby is getting enough milk if she seems sat-isfied, wets six to eight diapers a day, and gains weight steadily.

• If your nipples get sore, try coating them with organic olive oil between feedings. If that doesn't cut it, use lanolin.

• The American Academy of Pediatrics recommends that ba-bies be breast-fed exclusively for the first six months of life and in conjunction with solid foods until their first birthday. Longer, if you're both enjoying it.

• Once you get the hang of it, you'll practically be able to breast-feed while cooking dinner, talking on the phone, and spinning plates. In other words, it can be challenging at first, but stick with it and it'll get much easier.

• If you need support, contact a lactation consultant near you (www.ilca.org) or your local chapter of the La Leche League (www.llli.org).

• Try to allow ninety minutes between feedings, if you can stretch it that long. Otherwise, you may get sore and frus-trated, at least at first.

• One hidden benefit of breast-feeding exclusively: Your baby's poop won't stink. At least, not as badly!

Have Energy

. . .

"If you can nurse, do it. At least, at first. But if you can't
or you aren't successful, don't beat yourself up over it.
Your kid will turn out no matter what. Either way is fine.
Just do what works for you and your baby."

—CLAIRE BRIED

HOW TO KEEP EATING WELL FOR TWO

Step 1: Try to eat healthy. When you're nursing, all the nutrients you take in go straight to your breast milk first, and anything leftover stays with you. So, at every meal, aim to fill half your plate with fruits and veggies; that'll help give you iron (translation: energy) and the four hundred micrograms of folate you need a day to help your baby develop normally. Fill the other half of your plate with lean protein, like chicken or fish, and whole grains. And, if anyone ever asks if you've got a generous bone in your body, say, "Yes, I've got 206 of them." In order to fortify your milk, all 206 bones in your body hand over calcium to help make your baby strong. Reward them for this act and replenish their supply by eating three servings of low-fat dairy, or one thousand milligrams of calcium, a day.

Step 2: Have seconds. You'll need an additional three to five hundred calories to keep the liquid gold flowing, so go ahead, have that extra scoop of ice cream. If anyone questions you, go in for the martyr points and tell them you're doing it for the good of the baby.

Step 3: Indulge occasionally. Go ahead and enjoy that ice-cold beer or earthy cabernet you've been dreaming about for nine straight months. Just try to do it immediately after a feeding. Alcohol does indeed make its way into your breast milk, so you should wait two hours after that drink to nurse your baby again.

Step 4: Live in a no-honking zone. In other words, any foods that make you gassy will likely also make your baby gassy, so keep your black bean salsa, egg roll, and extra spicy guacamole intake to a minimum.

More Timeless Tips

- Your diet does affect the flavor of your breast milk, so if you want to raise an un-picky eater, try varying your meals as much as possible to expand his palate.

- Drink plenty of water. Adequate hydration only helps your milk supply.

- Steer clear of mercury-laden fish, like shark, swordfish, tilefish, and king mackerel. They could do a number on your baby's developing brain.

- Moderate caffeine drinking is fine, but if you notice your baby getting exceptionally fussy after your morning joe, try laying off the Starbucks for a while.

Up Your Stash

. . .

"I took three months off from work, and when I went back, I'd pump in the bathroom with a little handheld manual pump. The hardest part of working is that moment when you suddenly feel your breasts tingling. I can remember giving one presentation and I felt water on my feet. I thought, Is it raining in here? Then I looked down at my blouse and saw two wet spots. I went and put on my jacket and just carried on."

—Esther Safran Foer

HOW TO PUMP

Step 1: Wait two weeks. During your first fourteen days with your baby, your body is working hard to establish your milk supply at a Goldilocks level—that is, not too much, not too little, but just right. Once that's settled, feel free to start expressing milk so you can fill a bottle, head out of the house for a bit, and remember what it's like to be a normal person, or so you can simply give your partner a chance to feed (and bond with) the baby.

Step 2: Do it in the morning. Especially when your baby is eating every two hours, it's tough to even think about having surplus. Your best bet: Pump a half hour after your first morning feeding. If you're going to have any extra milk, that's when you'll most likely find it.

Step 3: Do it at night. Once your baby starts sleeping for longer stretches, you can squeeze in an extra pumping session after she goes down and before you do.

Step 4: Do it whenever she takes a bottle. If you have to go back to work, or be away from your baby for more than a few hours, it's important to trick your breasts into thinking you're still feeding her on a regular schedule. That way, your milk supply will remain consistent. So if she's chilling at home and drinking bottles all day and you're at work, then find a quiet, private place and pump whenever you'd normally feed her, probably about every three hours. (A new federal law requires that all workplaces give you time to pump for a year after your baby's birth, as well as a place to pump other than the bathroom.) Store the expressed milk in a portable cooler until you get home. Then transfer it to the fridge or freezer, where it can be stored until you're ready to use it.

More Timeless Tips

- If your breasts are engorged, pump for a few minutes to soften them and make latching on easier for your baby. Nobody can get a good grip on a couple of softballs.

- To encourage more milk production, try pumping immediately after a feeding. Emptying each breast fully will send the message that you need more milk now, and your body will respond.

- Any existential crises you might have sitting still, topless, and using both hands to hold two bottles to your breasts can be avoided by either buying a pumping bra or even better just hacking an old sports bra. Cut two holes in it for the flanges and voilà! Hands-free pumping!

- If you plan on pumping more than once a day, consider investing in a motorized breast pump, rather than a hand pump. And don't cheap out on it either. A good pump will save you so much time and frustration.

Stock Up

. . .

"I wasn't able to physically breast-feed my kids until they were two months old, because they were too little, so I had to pump and store my milk. What got me through was knowing they were getting that extra boost from me, and that was just what they needed. Keeping the right attitude about pumping is crucial. Otherwise, it sucks and you feel like a cow."

—Erinn McGurn

HOW TO STORE BREAST MILK

Step 1: Leave it out. If you know you're going to use the milk you've just expressed soon, simply keep the bottle on your countertop (or next to your bed or by the crib or even in your purse). It's good at room temperature for up to eight hours.

Step 2: Pop it in the fridge. Stow bottles you don't need right now, but will probably need tomorrow or the next day, in the refrigerator. They'll keep in the cool for up to five days.

Step 3: Freeze it. If you don't need the milk within a few hours or days, pour it into a freezer bag designed especially for breast milk, date it, mark how many ounces the bag contains, and toss it in the freezer. It'll be good to go for up to six months on ice.

More Timeless Tips

- Use fresh breast milk whenever possible, since cooling and freezing it destroys some of the antibodies.

- To avoid waste, store your milk in single-serving sizes, usually three to four ounces.

- It's OK to combine multiple pumpings into one bottle or bag. In the beginning you may only get a half-ounce or so at a time, so just add the next pumping's worth of milk to the same container until you get a good two ounces or so.

- Always use the oldest milk first.

- You may combine storage methods for one bottle. For example, after a few hours on the counter, you can move it to the fridge for five days. Still didn't use it? Just freeze it.

- Once you've thawed frozen milk, it cannot be refrozen. It'll keep in the fridge for twenty-four hours or at room temperature for one hour.

Warm Up

. . .

*"Oh, I enjoyed feeding my kids bottles. I'd sit in the rocking
chair and hold them real close, and they both loved eating.
It was a satisfying time for both of us."*

—Elaine Maddow

HOW TO WARM A BOTTLE

Step 1: Place the filled and chilled bottle in a mug or bowl.

Step 2: Tell your baby that it'll be just a few minutes more.
Warning: If he's crying, these few minutes will feel like the longest of your life, but don't worry. Sweet relief is on the way!

Step 3: Fill the bowl with hot water (straight from the faucet,
warmed in the microwave, or heated in a kettle) until it covers
the contents of the bottle, but not the nipple. You don't want any
water leaking in.

Step 4: Test it. Remove the bottle from the hot water, turn it
upside down, and shake a little milk onto the inside of your wrist.
It's ready when it feels like nothing—no warmer or colder than
your skin.

Step 5: Give it a swirl before serving. That'll help combat any separation that happened in the fridge, without adding any bubbles, which can give your baby gas.

More Timeless Tips

- Never microwave a bottle directly; even if the first few drops feel just right to you, there may be hidden hot spots within that can burn your baby's mouth.

- While babies love warmed bottles, most will take room temperature or cold bottles, too, especially if they're hungry enough.

Fill 'Er Up

. . .

"Oh, I enjoyed feeding my daughter. My husband did, too. He was wonderful. He was a great father and a great mother. When she'd wake up at night, we'd both race to take care of her, but he'd beat me all the time, because he was on the easy side of the bed."

—Ruth Alsop

HOW TO BOTTLE-FEED

Step 1: Look for hunger cues. Your baby will tell you when she needs to eat, and you should always feed her on demand. No, she won't hold her index finger in the air and give you a quick nod, but her signs will be just as obvious. She'll stick out her tongue, smack her lips, put her hands to her mouth, and get squirmy. If you miss all of these signals, she'll give you one that you can't ignore: a loud cry.

Step 2: Fill your bottle. If you're feeding your baby formula, mix up a single batch according to the instructions on the container. (Never add extra water or extra powder.) If you're using freshly expressed breast milk, then it's good-to-go as is. Either way, usually a couple of ounces per session will do the trick for a newborn; as your baby grows, so will the size of her meals.

Step 3: Cradle your baby. Hold your little one in an almost-upright position, so her head is supported in the crook of your elbow. If she's too horizontal, she could choke, and if she's too vertical, her noggin may flop forward.

Step 4: Feed her. Hold the bottle parallel to the floor and tip it only until the liquid just fills the nipple. (Any further, and the milk will come too fast.) Then, brush the nipple against your baby's lips until she opens her mouth and latches on. Never force it. If she doesn't open up, just try again later.

Step 5: Watch her. If liquid starts running out the sides of her mouth, she starts to flail, or her toes curl, you're feeding her too quickly. Give her a chance to catch her breath by either removing the bottle or tilting it back until she's ready to drink again. If she doesn't want to finish the bottle, don't make her. Conversely, if she gulps it down and still seems hungry, give her a pacifier for fifteen minutes. It takes just a little longer than that for the stomach to send the message to your brain that it's full. If she still acts hungry after fifteen minutes, offer her another bottle.

Step 6: Burp her. Bottle-fed babies tend to swallow more air than breast-fed babies, so relieve her of any gas by rubbing or patting her back once she finishes. To become an expert burper, see page 87.

More Timeless Tips

- Wash all your bottles, nipples included, according to the manufacturer's instructions before you use them for the first time.

- Start with a slow-flow nipple, so your baby can drink at her own pace. If she seems frustrated that the liquid isn't coming out fast enough, upgrade to a faster one.

- If your baby is crying but she ate within the past two hours, make sure her wails aren't due to a wet diaper, a burp, or a craving for cuddles. While feeding on demand will reduce her risk of obesity, you need to make sure you're responding to real hunger cues (and not just every ol' cry) with food. Crying is your baby's only way of telling you that she needs something, and more often than not, that something is not a bottle or your breast.

- Try not to overfeed your baby. Studies show overfeeding during infancy is often a precursor to obesity.

Pat Down

• • •

"Burp your baby halfway through the feeding and again at the end, and you'll have a good burper. My kids are still good burpers!"
—CHRISTINE SAMUEL

HOW TO BURP YOUR BABY

Step 1: Master your timing. Burp your baby after every ounce in the beginning, and after every two to three ounces after that. Also, go in for a burp mid-meal whenever he starts getting squirmy or fussy, or you switch sides while breast-feeding. Finally, burp your baby after every feeding, lest you be spit up on later.

Step 2: Get him into position. There are a few great ways to encourage any air he may have gulped to escape. Choose whichever one makes you—and him—most comfortable.

- The over-the-shoulder hold: Gently lay your baby against your chest, cupping his bottom with your hand and allowing his chin to settle on your shoulder.

- The lap hold: Sit down, if you haven't already. Then sit your baby on your thighs, facing either side and leaning slightly

forward. Hold him steady by supporting his chest with the palm of your hand and cradling his chin between your thumb and forefinger.

- The face-downer: Sit down and lay your baby, belly down, across your lap with his tummy resting on one thigh and his head, turned to either side, on the other.

Step 3: Go for it. Either rub upward on his back or gently pat between his shoulder blades with an open hand. (If you're doing the lap hold, you can also try just rocking him back and forth.)

Step 4: Repeat, as needed. Keep patting, rubbing, or rocking for a good five to ten minutes, changing positions, if you like. Still no burp? Then, as we say in Brooklyn, fuggedaboudit. There may not be one in there.

More Timeless Tips

- For extra oomph, try walking around or gently bouncing while burping. Often, the added up-and-down motion is all you need to coax stubborn air out.

- To reduce the amount (and volume) of burps, try to reduce the amount of air that your baby swallows in the first place. Make sure he gets a good latch. And if you're bottle-feeding, make sure there's liquid in the nipple when he starts sucking. Once the bottle is empty, take it away.

- If your babe zonks out after a meal, feel free to forgo the burping altogether. There's no need to mess with him when, clearly, he's as comfy as can be.

Log On

. . .

*"I was a nut about this! Especially with two babies, because I wanted
to remember that I'd fed them. Also, sometimes I fed them,
sometimes my husband did, and the log helped us keep track.
I kept that log until they were a year old! At some point,
it felt a little silly, but it was always helpful. And now it's
an amazing record of their first year of life. To see how
when they came home, they could only eat an ounce
at a time, and by nine months they could eat
six ounces!"*

—Erinn McGurn

HOW TO KEEP A DAILY RECORD OF INS AND OUTS

Step 1: Get a notebook and pen. During the first two weeks of
life, your baby needs to eat about every two hours around the clock
(from the *start* of one feeding to the next), and you need to track
her progress to make sure she's doing all right. Exhaustion will
turn your mind to mush, so it's best to rely on old-fashioned pen
and paper.

Step 2: Write the date at the top of the page.

Step 3: Make four columns across the top: start time, finish
time, side/ounces, diaper.

Step 4: Record the goings-on. Jot down the minute you start feeding, the minute you finish, and either an "L" (for left) or an "R" (for right), depending on which breast she ate from. (You'll always start the next feeding from the side you last ended on to ensure equal milk production in both breasts.) Or if you're feeding her formula, just track how many ounces she eats and when. Finally, whenever you change her diaper, put a "W" for wet and/or a "D" for dirty (or "P" for poopy, if you so desire).

Step 5: Review her progress every day. If she's breast-feeding, she'll need to eat eight to twelve times a day, for at least ten minutes a pop, for the first two weeks. If she's eating formula, she'll eat two to three ounces per session. As far as diapers go, you're ultimately aiming for at least six wet ones and three dirty ones a day. But for the first few days, expect as many pees and poops as the number of days she is old. So, on day one, she should pee and poop once each. On day two, she should pee and poop twice each. Her poop will top out on day three (three pees, three poops), and her wet ones will top out on day six (six pees, three poops).

More Timeless Tips

- Use a pen (or pencil) that doesn't roll, so when you ham-handedly reach for it in the middle of the night, it won't immediately fall onto the floor.

- If you don't have a digital clock that lights up, get one. That'll save you from struggling to make out the time in the middle of the night.

- Keep your log until you feel confident that all of your baby's systems are go. For some parents, two weeks may be enough. For others, it may take two months. Do whatever gives you peace of mind.

Toot Toot

. . .

"Mother always said when a baby would cry, it was either hungry or had a bellyache. So I'd rock my girls and hold them and put them on their backs. Usually it was a burp."

—BETTY HORTON

HOW TO HELP A GASSY BABY

Step 1: Relax. Burping and tooting a lot is part of life as a baby. Neither is a sign of trouble, so when you hear your baby let one rip, smile, feel a little proud that you've got such a robust child, and then move on with your day. His digestive system is still getting up and running. Plus, he's inevitably going to swallow air while eating and crying, and that air has got to come out one way or another.

Step 2: Burp him. It's your best bet for getting any air bubbles in his belly o-u-t. Just rub upward on or gently pat his back. (For other no-fail burping tips, see page 87.)

Step 3: Give him tummy time. Lay him, belly-down, across your knees, using one hand to support his head and the other to gently rub his back. Or if you'd rather stand, lay him, belly-down, across your body, on your forearm. (You can rest his head in the crook of your elbow or in the palm of your hand.) Sometimes a little pressure on his tum-tum is what it takes to soothe him.

Step 4: Bicycle his legs. If the gas seems to be headed south, rather than north, lay him on his back and move his legs around as if he's pedaling a bike. Bending his legs toward his belly often provides relief, allowing any toots he has at the ready to escape.

Step 5: Hold him upright and walk. Or bounce on a big exercise ball if you've got one. The up-and-down motion, coupled with the pressure of your bodies against each other, can coax any trapped air out (in *either* of you, by the way).

More Timeless Tips

- Help him swallow less air in the first place by making sure he has a good latch when breast-feeding, or that there's plenty of milk or formula in the nipple when bottle-feeding.

- Don't wait until he's howling to feed him. Pay attention to his early hunger cues and respond accordingly. That way, he'll be less ravenous and therefore less likely to suck wind with his meal.

- Watch your diet if you're breast-feeding, and avoid any foods, like broccoli or cabbage, that may cause you to pass gas not only on your own, but also to your baby.

Chow Down

• • •

*"Their food would get all over everything. I'd put a spoonful in
their mouth, and they'd razz it all over. Green beans are real nice to do
that to. But, I'd just wipe 'em up and keep going."*

—MARY HUFF

HOW TO INTRODUCE YOUR BABY TO SOLIDS

Step 1: Time it right. The American Academy of Pediatrics
recommends that babies breast-feed exclusively for about the first
six months of life. But if your peanut has celebrated her four-
month birthday, can sit up on her own, gets a ravenous look on
her face when you sit down to dinner, and starts to actually grab
for your baby-back ribs, then you know she's ready for the next
step.

Step 2: Get the gear. Technically, you could plunk her in her car seat or swing (if it has a seat lock) to eat, but things are going to get pretty messy pretty fast. So if you don't want your car or living room to smell like pureed peas, invest in a high chair stat. And while you're at it, pick up some soft rubber or plastic spoons and bibs. Lots and lots of bibs. (Or you can make your own; see page 163.)

Step 3: Make her menu. Whether you serve her oatmeal, apple-sauce, sweet potatoes, or just about any other fruit, vegetable, or grain makes no difference. Babies are born with a preference for sweets, and you can't do a darn thing about it. So chill, Mama. Starting her on pureed pears, rather than peas, won't make her a vegetable-hating sugar addict. (And in fact, if you only feed her foods she's less likely to enjoy, she may not like to eat much at all.) The only three things you need to keep in mind right now: (1) In-troduce her to only one new food at a time, waiting four to five days between each before branching out. That way, if she has an aller-gic reaction, you'll know exactly what caused it. (2) Steer clear of foods that are more likely to cause allergic reactions, like peanuts, soy, wheat, shellfish, fish, milk, and eggs. (3) Never give honey to a baby under a year. Got it? Easy.

Step 4: Check in with your baby. Morning, afternoon, or night, it doesn't matter when you feed her first. Just catch her when she's in a great mood, like after a long night's snooze or a solid after-noon nap.

Step 5: Prepare the food. Either make your own (see page 98 for instructions) or pop a jar. Serving it at room temperature may go over just fine, but if you prefer to heat it (in the microwave or in a bowl of hot water), stir it well and test it on your own tongue to make sure there are no hot spots. You don't need a lot. For her first time out, she'll only eat a couple of teaspoons. (Within two to three months, she'll be eating three meals a day, at two to four tablespoons a pop, plus breast milk or formula.)

Step 6: Set her up. Strap her into her high chair and bib her up.

Step 7: Spoon it up. Until now, your baby has never swallowed anything but milk or formula, so make her first attempt easy by giving her only a little bit on the tip of the spoon. Give her time to get used to it, and once she swallows it (or at least some of it), give her another taste. If food dribbles onto her chin, scoop it up with the spoon for the next go-round.

Step 8: Let her tell you when she's finished. She's not going to put her finger up in the air, raise her eyebrows, and mouth the words, "Check, please," so you've got to pay attention to her other cues. If she turns her head away or locks her lips, the meal is over.

More Timeless Tips

- Thin her first foods with breast milk or formula, until they are an almost watery consistency. It'll help your baby figure out how to get the food to the back of her throat and swallow it without choking.

- If she immediately pushes every bit of food back out of her mouth as soon as you put it in, don't get frustrated. She may simply have not yet lost her tongue-thrust reflex, which helps babies drink from a bottle or breast. (It usually fades out around four months.) Be patient and try again tomorrow or the next day.

Mix It Up

...

*"I had a little blender. It was just so much easier.
One carrot and you're done!"*
—Sunchita Tyson

HOW TO MAKE YOUR OWN BABY FOOD

Step 1: Buy organic fruits and veggies. Good starters: apples, pears, sweet potatoes, and peas. They're all easy on the belly.

Step 2: Steam 'em. Remove the skin, if necessary, and chop into small chunks. Then toss your fruit or veggie into a steamer basket, lower it into a pot or pan with about an inch of boiling water, and cover.

Step 3: Cook until tender. Peas take as little as three minutes. Apples can take up to twelve. Test for doneness with a fork. If the food is soft and mashes easily, continue to Step 4. If it's still chunky or hard, cook it a little longer.

Step 4: Cool.

Step 5: Puree. Toss your fruit or veggie into a food processor or blender. If it's too thick for your little one, thin it out with some breast milk or formula, until it's a consistency she can handle.

Step 6: Serve.

More Timeless Tips

- Never add salt or sugar to your baby's meals. Your baby doesn't need it, and her digestive system may not be ready for it.

- Some fruits, like ripe bananas or avocados, don't require any steaming. Just puree and serve.

- As your baby gets older, you can get more creative in your cooking by combining two or more ingredients, including meat. Try chicken and apples, apples and butternut squash, and even ricotta and kale. Taste it first. If you like it, chances are your baby will too.

- Made too much? As long as you haven't or your baby hasn't double dipped a spoon, you can pour the extra into an ice cube tray, freeze, and store the individual serving sizes in a plastic bag.

- No time? Just pop a jar of store-bought organic baby food. There are some great ones out there made with 100 percent fruit or veggies and no additives or preservatives.

4

Comforting

. . .

Learn to soothe your child now,
and you'll build a bond for life.

Bundle Up

. . .

"I had my kids really swaddled. I figured,
If it was good enough for the baby Jesus,
it was good enough for them."

—SUNCHITA TYSON

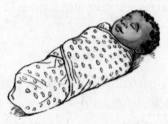

HOW TO SWADDLE

Step 1: Spread a small blanket diagonally on a safe flat surface, like a changing table or bed.

Step 2: Fold the top corner down about six inches.

Step 3: Lay the baby on the blanket, so the fold is just above the baby's shoulders and the bottom point is in line with his toes. Say coochie-coo.

Step 4: Gently holding the baby's right arm to his side, pull the right side of the blanket across the baby, tucking the corner beneath his bottom.

Step 5: Leaving enough room for the baby's hips to move up and out and also for his legs to extend if he wishes, fold up the bottom point of the blanket toward the baby's chin. If the blanket is too long, fold the bottom point down, so it's not covering the baby's face.

Step 6: Gently holding the baby's left arm to his side, pull the left corner of the blanket across him and tuck beneath his bottom.

Step 7: Pick him up and give him a sweet kiss.

More Timeless Tips

- If you've got a particularly wild baby, good luck! Leave his arms free by folding down the top corner farther and aligning the fold under his armpits. When you fold up the bottom corner, secure it by tucking it into the other folds at the top.

- Newborns like to be swaddled tightly around their arms and chest because it most resembles the womb and therefore makes them feel more secure. However, as your baby gets older, he may actually wake himself up trying to free himself from the swaddle. It's better, then, to leave his arms free so he can explore his world, suck his fingers, and (hopefully) soothe himself back to sleep.

- Always remember to leave enough room for his hips to move up and out, since a tight swaddle around his legs could cause hip dysplasia, or loose hip joints.

Scoop Poop

· · ·

*"Both of my kids were squirmy kids, so I'd sing
'Rock-a-bye Baby' to them, every time I changed them.
That helped."*

—CHRISTINE SAMUEL

HOW TO CHANGE A DIAPER

Step 1: Gather your supplies. You'll need a new diaper, some wipes, and petroleum jelly or ointment, if necessary.

Step 2: Find a good spot. Lay the baby down on a clean, flat surface, and talk to her. Just because you're doing dirty work doesn't mean it's not a great time to bond. Besides, it's much easier changing the diaper of a calm baby than a crying baby.

Step 3: Assess the situation. Unfasten the dirty diaper and take a peek at what happened inside.

Step 4: Free her up. Gently lift up the baby's bottom by carefully grasping both of her ankles with one hand. Then fold the diaper in half, so the clean outside of the front is directly under her tush. Once she's in the clear, lower her down.

Step 5: Clean her up. Using a clean, moist wipe, wash the baby's bottom. Wipe girls from front to back to prevent infection. (Wipe boys all over.) Once she's clean, toss the dirty diaper and wipes.

Step 6: Lift her up once more, same way, and slide a new diaper underneath, making sure the sticky tabs are behind her, facing up.

Step 7: Apply petroleum jelly if her bottom looks A-OK. It acts as a barrier to help prevent irritation. If her bottom looks red, or if she has diaper rash, apply ointment or cream.

Step 8: Fasten the diaper by folding the front half toward her belly. Then, open the tabs on the bottom and affix them to the front. The diaper should be snug but not tight.

More Timeless Tips

- Often, the cool air on a baby's bum will trigger her tinkler system, so work quickly.

- Never leave your baby unattended on a changing table, and always keep one hand on her so she doesn't roll off.

- If the baby still has an umbilical cord, fold the front of the diaper down, so it's not pressing on the cord.

- Keep a toy nearby to entertain and distract your baby.

- If you're changing a boy, wear swimming goggles, or better yet, keep a clean washcloth handy to avoid accidental spurts. Also, point his wee down before closing the diaper, so he'll stay dry.

Cradle Softly

• • •

"You have to be gentle with babies,
but they're not going to break."

—MARY HUFF

HOW TO HOLD A BABY

For Newborns

Step 1: Give him support. While leaning over your baby as far as you can, gently slide one hand, fingers spread, under his head and neck and the other hand, fingers spread, under his tush. Since his little neck isn't yet strong enough to support his head, you've got to do it for him.

Step 2: Scoop him up. Without moving your hands from their supportive positions, bend over him and lift him toward your torso, so his tiny body, head included, rests on your chest, and then straighten yourself up. You can stop here if you're both comfy, or proceed to Step 3.

Step 3: Cradle him in your arms. Always supporting his head, gently lay him down in your arm so his head is resting in the crook of your elbow and his bottom is snug in your hand. Use the other hand to give him extra support and cuddles.

For Older Babies (Who Can Support Their Own Heads)

The extrovert: For the baby who doesn't want to miss any action, turn him so he's facing out and hold him vertically in front of you against your chest. Place your left hand beneath his bottom, your right arm across his chest, and your right hand supporting him underneath his armpit. This is also a good hold for friends and relatives to employ; if your baby can keep an eye on you, he'll likely be less fussy when being held by others.

The lounger: Hold your baby horizontally in front of you, allowing him to lie, face out, across your left forearm. Use your left hand to gently grip him between his legs. (His head will be nestled in the crook of your left elbow.) Add your right arm on top for more support. Because this hold applies light pressure to his belly, it can often put even gassy babies to sleep.

Other Timeless Tips

- Newborns startle very easily. Before picking up a baby, talk to him and gently rub his back or belly for a few seconds.

- Be smooth, never sudden or jerky, with your actions, or you'll have a crying baby on your hands.

- If you're a nervous wreck, just stay calm and know that it's up to you to make the infant feel secure and warm. The more you become comfortable holding him, the more he'll become comfortable being held by you. Stick with it.

- Your baby knows you not only by touch and sound, but also by smell. Let him nuzzle into you, and you'll soon find it's more challenging to put him down than it is to pick him up.

Swing Low

• • •

*"Can I summon the words to help me describe how I felt rocking
my kids? Sometimes, my children help me find the words. In one of
Jonathan's books, he talks about a man who'd taken a baby in,
and apparently the baby was wrapped in a Jewish newspaper,
and the man would hug her at night and read her from
right to left. That really resonated with me. I'd hug my kids
and look at them and try to figure out who they'd become
and how I could do the best job getting them there."*

—ESTHER SAFRAN FOER

HOW TO ROCK YOUR BABY

Step 1: Cradle her in your arms. Her head should be nestled
in the crook of your elbow and her bottom supported by your
hand. Use your other arm for added support beneath her bottom
and back.

Step 2: Bring her close. Your babe has spent the past nine
months in a very snug womb, so don't leave her out there dangling. Hold her tightly against you, so she feels secure. Also,
hold her close to your face, so she can actually focus on you. (For
the first month of life, babies have 20/120 vision, which means, if
given an eye test, they'd only be able to see the big "E" at the top
of the chart. By eight months, their vision is much closer to that
of an adult.)

Step 3: Sway. With your feet shoulder-width apart and knees slightly bent, slowly shift your weight from side to side.

More Timeless Tips

- To seal your bond, look your baby in the eyes while rocking her.

- If your baby is particularly fussy, add a squat, or deep-knee bend, while you sway. The swooping motion almost always calms cries.

- If your arms and legs get tired (and they will), invest in a large exercise ball. When it's inflated, you can sit on it and gently rock without shredding your thighs. Your baby will love the bouncing and you'll get a good core workout, too.

- Or, you know, you can just sit in a rocking chair or glider.

Sing to Sleep

. . .

"I can't sing for cold beans, but I always sang to my girls."
—BETTY HORTON

HOW TO SING A LULLABY

Step 1: Let go of your expectations. You don't have to be an American Idol to sing a lullaby. After all, it's the comforting sound of your soft and familiar voice, not your perfect pitch, that will soothe your baby to sleep.

Step 2: Choose a tune. The moment you decide to sing to your baby is almost always the moment that the lyrics and melody of every single song you've ever known will leave your head. So, here are a few easy lullabies to keep in your back pocket.

Twinkle, Twinkle Little Star

Twinkle, twinkle, little star
How I wonder what you are
Up above the world so high,
Like a diamond in the sky.
Twinkle, twinkle, little star
How I wonder what you are.

Brahms's Lullaby

Lullaby and good night
With roses bedight
With lilies bedecked
Is baby's wee bed

Lay thee down now and rest
May thy slumber be blessed
Lay thee down now and rest
May thy slumber be blessed.

Rock-a-bye Baby

Rock-a-bye baby, in the treetop
When the wind blows, the cradle will rock
When the bough breaks, the cradle will fall
And down will come baby, cradle and all.

***Step 3*:** Let 'er rip. Keeping your voice soft and steady, simply start your song, preferably while also rocking your baby. As he begins to drift off, take your volume down a notch. Have faith that he'll be asleep in no time, and you can soon follow.

More Timeless Tips

• Make sure your baby is fed, changed, and dressed for sleep before bringing out the lullabies.

• If you forget the lyrics to, well, everything, allow your stream of consciousness to take over and simply sing whatever you're doing to the tune of "Brahms's Lullaby," even if it's *"Close your eyes, go to sleep, my sweet darling baby, 'cause it's nighttime, time for sleeping, and you have to go to sleep."* Or, change the words to "Rock-a-bye Baby": *"Rock-a-bye baby, in the treetop, if you don't sleep, my head will soon pop, then after that, my head will explode, and that won't be good, baby, no good at all."*

- You may not win any Grammys, but that's not the point. Singing softly, whatever the song, is. And luckily, he can't yet understand the words, so the pressure's off to come up with brilliant lyrics.

Make Peace

. . .

"You know that saying 'Put your own air mask on before you put on theirs?' Well, when we get ourselves calm, that's when the baby starts getting calm."

—ROSEMARY GIUNTA

HOW TO SOOTHE A CRYING BABY

Step 1: Pick her up. If your baby starts fussing, she may simply want you. Cuddle her in your arms, rock her, or even strap her on in a baby carrier. Feeling your touch, smelling your skin, and hearing your heartbeat could be all it takes to calm her. However, if it's not, don't worry. It's not because you're a lousy parent; it's because she's simply trying to tell you something and doesn't have the words for it. You're doing fine. Just run down the checklist step by step, and you'll both feel better in no time.

Step 2: Check her diaper. Nobody likes sitting in wet (or worse, poopy) pants, and crying is one of the only ways your little peach can tell you so. If it's dirty, yeah, you know what to do.

Step 3: Burp her. Gas is often a likely culprit, so rub her back in an upward motion or give it some gentle pats. (For more tips on burping, see page 87.) Oftentimes, she'll let one rip and then immediately quiet down. If you suspect the gas is traveling downward, help her toot it out by laying her down on her back and bicycling her legs. (For more ideas on calming a gassy baby, see page 93.) If you think she just has an upset tummy, hold her facedown, or on her left side, across your forearm, to help aid her digestion.

Step 4: Check her skin. Babies will fuss if they're either too warm or too chilly. Are her fingers and toes ice cubes? Is her forehead moist with sweat? Add or remove a layer accordingly.

Step 5: Assess her environment. She could be overstimulated, especially if her three-year-old cousin, who just happens to *love, love, love* babies, is all up in her grill. If that's the case, take your baby into a quiet room and let her have some space and downtime. Or, conversely, she could be understimulated. If you suspect she's bored out of her mind, talk to her, play with her, read her a book, or give her a toy. Finally, she may just be in need of a dose of fresh air. Take her for a short walk, even if it's to the end of the driveway. The change of scenery may be all she needs.

Step 6: Check if she's hungry. If you missed all of her early cues—smacking her lips, chomping on her fingers, opening her mouth, and looking for boob or bottle—she'll give you a signal you cannot ignore. Crying is her last-ditch way of telling you she's hungry, so offer her something to eat. (You may have to calm her down a bit first by rocking or shushing her, since it can be tough for your little one to latch on when she's howling. While crying, your babe's tongue presses against the roof of her mouth, which makes it difficult to stick a bottle or breast in there.)

Step 7: Help her sleep. Haven't you had nights (or even days) when you've been so exhausted that you just want to cry? Your baby may lack the skills to soothe herself to sleep, even when she's totally beat, so step in and help her out. Hold her, give her a bath, swaddle her (it helps her feel secure), rock her, sing to her, give her a massage, and/or give her something to suck on, like her hand, your little finger, or a pacifier. Once she's chill, set her down in her crib, bouncer, swing, or even her car seat and watch her drift off to la-la land.

Step 8: Return to Step 1. When all else fails, go back to the beginning and start again. Sometimes babies don't know why they're crying, and sometimes there isn't even a reason, other than that they're just—there's no better word—pissed that they're not back in their cozy, dark womb. Stay calm, and help your baby get to know and love this crazy world of ours.

More Timeless Tips

- Sometimes scratchy tags, a too-tight diaper, even one of your hairs wrapped around her finger or toe will send her into fits of hysteria. So if you have no idea why she's crying and you've tried everything else, give her a once-over with your go-go-gadget eye and look for small annoyances.

- Make some noise. Sound can often offer comfort, so try gently shh-ing her, singing to her, playing her some music, turning on a white noise machine, or running the vacuum cleaner.

- Get moving. Sometimes a walk around the block or a short car ride will lull her to sleep. Or, if you can't leave the house, try holding her tight and either bouncing your knees or—seriously—doing squats. That almost always works, and you'll get killer quads to boot! Too pooped? Sit on a large exercise ball and gently bounce up and down.

- Rule out something more serious. No matter how frazzled you feel, remember that feistiness in babies is almost always a good sign; it's much less worrisome than, say, listlessness. Even so, call your doctor if any of the following symptoms appear: She gets a fever, refuses to eat, wheezes, vomits, gets diarrhea, sports a rash, or hasn't had a wet diaper in more than six hours.

- If she won't stop bawling and you're ready to lose your mind, set her down in a safe space, like her crib, and walk away for a few minutes. Take a shower, call your mom, take a few deep breaths, and then try soothing her again, and before you know it, you'll both be calm. Just whatever you do, never, *ever* shake a baby. Your momentary snap could cause serious brain damage or even death.

- All babies are angels, but some are particularly happy from the start and some are colicky and cry all the time. Most likely, yours will fall somewhere in between. Whichever kind of baby you get, try to enjoy this time together as much as you can, even if it happens to be particularly noisy, because it won't last forever.

Feel Kneaded

. . .

*"We'd rub their backs before bed. I think it was very comforting
for them and helped them sleep. You want to let them
know that you're connected to them."*

—Elaine Maddow

HOW TO GIVE A BABY MASSAGE

Step 1: Set the mood. Lay your baby down on a blanket or
towel on a flat, comfy surface in a cozy room, making sure there
are no drafts. And master your timing, too. Try a massage immediately following bathtime and before bed, when she's quiet
and calm. It may help her nod off.

Step 2: Undress your baby. You can have her completely nekkid,
if you're daring, or in nothing but her diaper. Once she's ready,
lay her, faceup, on the towel, lay your (hopefully warm) hands
on her chest and belly, smile at her, and talk to her in your most
soothing voice.

Step 3: Start with her noodle. Place your thumbs on her forehead and gently work your way out toward her temples. Then
place them alongside the bridge of her nose and work your way
along her cheekbones back toward her temples. Gently rub her

ears between your thumbs and pointers. Finally, gently run your fingers along her jaw toward her chin.

Step 4: Lotion up. Once your doc gives you the OK to use lotion (it could irritate a *very* young baby's skin), you can use any kind of safe, non-irritating oil or lotion you'd like. Squirt some in your hands and rub them together to warm it up. If you don't have anything fancy, olive oil will do. Just be warned: Using it may trigger intense cravings for Italian food.

Step 5: Massage her chest and belly. Place your fingertips on her sternum and rub outward toward her shoulders. Then gently rub her tummy in a circular motion, moving clockwise.

Step 6: Do her arms. Wrap your pointer and thumb around her upper arm and, squeezing gently, work your way toward her hand, enlisting your other hand along the way. Finish by gently squeezing and tugging each of her fingers. Switch sides and repeat.

Step 7: Do her legs. Use the same technique you used on her arms, working your way from her upper thigh to her feet and finishing by squeezing each toe.

Step 8: Rub her back. Roll her over so she's on her tummy and, using both hands, stroke from side to side, top to bottom. Then, using your fingertips, make small circular motions working your way from the center of her upper back out to her shoulders. Finally, give her heinie cheeks a couple of good rounds.

Step 9: Finish with a kiss.

More Timeless Tips

- This is a baby massage, not a Swedish massage. Use a gentle touch, not a heavy hand. It should be only firm enough not to tickle or itch your baby.

- Steer clear of your baby's spine. You're being a masseuse, not a chiropractor. Same goes for the soft spots on her head, obviously.

- Let your baby lead you. If she's not into it, don't force it. Just try again another time. And if she's loving it, keep going. You'll probably enjoy giving the massage as much as she enjoys getting it.

Get Cheeky

...

"It's scary, but of course, you never let go of that thermometer.
Vaseline 'em up, and never let go of that thermometer."

—Claire Bried

How to take a rectal temperature

Step 1: Lay your baby facedown, across your lap or on a flat surface, like his changing table, and place your hand on his back to prevent him from rolling over.

Step 2: Lube your thermometer. Place a bit of petroleum jelly or olive oil on the tip to help ease it in.

Step 3: Take a deep breath. Know that this will be harder for you than it will for your baby. He'll hardly feel it, so chill, Mama. It's going to be just fine.

Step 4: Stick it in. Place your thumb on the thermometer about a quarter to a half inch from the tip, and then slide the tip into his bottom no farther than your thumb. (If you hit resistance, stop—obviously.) Hold it in place until your thermometer beeps. It will feel like an eternity, but it should only take about a minute.

Step 5: Pull it out. Once you're through, read the number in the window. A normal temperature is 98.6. If it reads 100.4 or higher in your newborn, 101 or higher in your three- to six-month-old, or 103 or higher in your baby of any age, call your pediatrician immediately.

More Timeless Tips

- Digital thermometers are safer than the old-school glass ones, which contain mercury. The silver stuff is poisonous, and if the thermometer should break while you're taking a temp, that could spell big trouble.

- Never use a rectal thermometer in your baby's mouth, even if you've washed it a million times. Buy an oral thermometer or use a digital one that comes with different tips.

- Once your baby can hold a thermometer under her tongue, you can take her temperature orally. The readings you'll get from her heinie or mouth are much more accurate than one from her forehead or armpit.

- If you'd prefer to take her temperature faceup, lay her on her back, bend her legs toward her chest, and use one hand to hold the back of her thighs and the other to insert the thermometer.

Chew Out

· · ·

"That was rough, the poor little things. I kept teething rings in the refrigerator, and I'd rub their gums. I'd feel so sorry for them, but when their tooth came through, we'd take pictures."

—Sunchita Tyson

How to Calm a Teething Baby

Step 1: Watch for symptoms. Most babies spring their first pearly white, usually on the bottom, sometime between four and seven months. You'll know it's coming if you notice your baby drooling like a faucet, gnawing on everything in sight, pulling on his ears, crying more than usual, sleeping less than usual, or sporting swollen or red gums.

Step 2: Give him something to bite. Pressure on his gums helps soothe the pain, so offer him your finger, a cold, wet washcloth, or a rubber teething ring or toy.

Step 3: Massage his gums. Rub your pointer finger back and forth over gums for temporary relief. Just don't forget to wash your hands first.

More Timeless Tips

- Chill your teething ring in the fridge before handing it to your baby. The cold can help numb his gums. Just don't freeze the ring, or it could get too hard and when he chomps, he could injure his little gums.

- Over-the-counter numbing medications aren't worth the few bucks they cost, since they'll wash out of his mouth almost as soon as you rub them on his gums. Also, if you give him too much or miss your mark, you could do more harm than good.

- Teething can be a trying time, but before you know it, your little one will be smacking and cracking grape Bubblicious. Oh wait, that can be a trying time, too.

Kiss Good Night

...

*"We had a routine. They went to bed at the same time
every night. They'd have a bottle, and then we'd read them a story.
Then we'd put on the same music every night and put them down awake,
so they could put themselves to sleep. And by some miracle it worked!"*

—Erinn McGurn

HOW TO PUT YOUR BABY TO SLEEP

Step 1: Be at her beck and call for two months. For the first eight weeks of life, your baby will be on no set schedule. In fact, she won't even know day from night, and she's just so little that you need to feed her on demand at least every two hours. It's tough, but you'll be surprised how quickly you can get used to it. Try to squeeze in your own shut-eye whenever you can get it.

Step 2: Create a bedtime ritual. Once she's eight weeks, you can start to encourage good sleep habits. So, about a half hour before her bedtime, give her a warm bath, massage her, feed her, listen to soothing music, and read her a book, all of which should calm her down. When you do the same thing around the same time night after night, she'll soon learn what to expect.

Step 3: Respond to her sleepy signals. Watch for her heavy eyelids, floppy limbs, and that zoned-out look, and as soon as you see her getting tired, lay her down—always on her back—in her crib. Your goal: find that sweet spot when she's too drowsy to protest but awake enough to know what's going on. You want her to learn to fall asleep on her own, and if you hold, rock, or nurse her until it's lights-out, she won't gain that essential skill anytime soon. (And, later, when she wakes up in the night, she won't be able to put herself back to sleep without you.)

Step 4: Kiss her good night, and tell her you love her.

Step 5: Hold your breath. That's about all you can do. Only when your baby reaches fifteen to eighteen pounds, usually around four months, is she physically able to sleep through the night without any midnight (or 1 A.M., 2 A.M., 3 A.M., or 4 A.M.) snacks. That's when she has enough extra chub to metabolically make it for longer than a few hours without eating and still have enough energy to maintain her temperature and grow. Try not to respond to every little whimper, and hope she soothes herself back to sleep. There will be nights when she doesn't, and so, in advance, you and your partner must decide how you'll respond to her heartrending cries. Do you get her right away? Do you wait ten minutes, then go in and talk to her and pat her (without picking her up) and repeat, waiting five minutes longer between intervals, until she falls asleep? Or do you simply not respond at all? Each comes with its own pros and cons. Just know this: Ultimately, you and your baby will be happier when you both sleep through the night. Good luck!

More Timeless Tips

- The more you play with her during the day, the more likely she'll be ready to conk out at night. Limit her daytime naps to two hours, and don't let her nod off too close to bedtime either.

- Focus on her nighttime sleeping. Once she gets the hang of that, good naps will follow automatically.

- If your baby is acting fussy, that probably means she's over-tired. Try putting her down a little earlier tomorrow.

- If you do decide to console her if she wakes in the night, consider sending your partner in instead, especially if you're breast-feeding. Babies can smell their mom's milk, and it may be frustrating to her to know you're so close but not offering her any nom-noms. If your sweetie goes instead, all three of you may get back to sleep faster.

5

Polishing

. . .

*There's nothing more adorable than a baby, except
maybe a baby wrapped in a hooded towel,
fresh out of the bathtub.*

Rub-a-Dub

. . .

"Bathtime was always a playful time. David and Rachel both loved baths. They'd splash around. Later, they both joined the swim team when they were very young."

—ELAINE MADDOW

HOW TO GIVE A BATH

Step 1: Get everything ready. You'll need: a washcloth, a hooded baby towel, some gentle baby soap, a cup (for pouring water over your baby), a fresh diaper, and a clean outfit.

Step 2: Fill the tub. You can use a portable baby tub, or you can use your regular ol' bathtub (or even your kitchen sink), if you line the bottom with a baby bath-sponge, towel, or mat. You only need a couple of inches of warm water, about one hundred degrees. Test the temperature with your wrist or elbow to make sure it's not too hot or cold.

Step 3: Undress your little one and yell, "Naked baby!" There's nothing quite so delicious in this world as that oh-so-tiny tush.

Step 4: Ease him into the water, making sure to support his head all along. As you lower him, talk to him and smile at him, letting him know that what he's about to experience will be awesome and not at all scary.

Step 5: Clean him up. Wash his face with a washcloth. Then squirt some soap on the washcloth and lather him up, working from his cleanest parts to his dirtiest. To wash his back, you'll have to sit him up; just remember that he'll be slippery, so get a good grip on him by placing your arm across his chest and holding him beneath his armpit.

Step 6: Shampoo his hair. Gently massage soap into his scalp and then rinse it out, using your cup of water, taking care not to get soap in his eyes. You don't have to shampoo every day; two to three times a week should suffice, unless he's had a major spit-up incident, where it dribbles into his hair. Hey, it happens to the best of us.

Step 7: Finish up. Once he's all clean (and done playing), wrap him in a towel, pat him dry, diaper him, and get him dressed.

More Timeless Tips

- The key to a happy bath: Keep your baby warm by continuously pouring water over his arms, belly, and legs. And let him splash around to his heart's content. The more he enjoys his tubby now, the fewer battles you'll have down the road.

- Always be sure to wash in every crease, especially in the folds of his neck, thighs, and bottom, and even between his fingers and toes. You'd be amazed by how much lint gets caught there.

- Make a bath part of your baby's bedtime ritual. The warm water will calm him down before sleep. Also, try a tubby whenever your baby is especially gassy or cranky.

- If it's chilly in the room, turn on a hot shower to steam things up before drawing the baby's bath.

- Once your baby is in the water, never, ever walk away from the tub, even for just a split second.

- Until your baby's umbilical cord falls off, which can take a couple of weeks, you can only give him a sponge bath. (Same goes until his circumcision heals.) Here's how: Undress him down to the diaper, wrap him in a towel, and lay him on a flat surface, like his changing table or your bed. Wash his face with a wet washcloth first. Then, dip the washcloth into a bowl of warm, soapy water and work your way from his head to his toes, keeping the rest of his body covered with the towel as you go. Save his parts for last, and be quick about it, or you may have to start all over again.

Mouth Off

...

"We started brushing their gums at six months. It was to clean their mouths and get them used to brushing, but they also loved that pressure on their gums when they were teething."
—Erinn McGurn

How to Brush Baby Teeth (or Gums)

Step 1: Get comfy. Hold your baby on your lap and find a position where you both can relax.

Step 2: Slip on a rubber finger-toothbrush or use a soft-bristled infant toothbrush, dipped in water. You are your baby's first defense against tooth decay, which can start as soon as her first tooth pops up, so don't be a slacker.

Step 3: Rub down her teeth and gums, making sure you clean all sides. She'll likely open up and start chewing on your finger, which is just fine, if her chomping helps get the job done.

More Timeless Tips

- Set a good habit. Even before your babe sprouts a tooth, she's got gums, which need to be kept clean. After each feeding, wipe 'em down with a damp baby washcloth. A few quick swipes will clear away any plaque, which could harm her pearly whites as soon as they make their grand entrance.

- When your baby turns two and knows how to spit, use a pea-sized squirt of fluoridated, kid-friendly toothpaste on the brush. Before then, you may use a non-fluoridated training toothpaste, available at any drugstore.

- Schedule your baby's first dental visit when her first tooth appears and no later than her first birthday.

Brush Off

• • •

*"I had to scrub your head with a soft brush. It's just a waxy build up.
It's not like people were like, 'Ew, what's on your baby's head?'"*

—CLAIRE BRIED

HOW TO DEAL WITH CRADLE CAP

Step 1: Diagnose it. If you notice scaly, flaky patches on your baby's noggin, chances are it's cradle cap. Though doctors don't know why some kids get it and others don't, they suspect it has something to do with the hormones passed from mom to baby in the womb, which can kick your baby's oil glands into overdrive. It's nothing to worry about and it'll usually clear up on its own, but you can also help it along.

Step 2: Get greasy. Rub a few drops of organic olive oil onto his scalp, let it sit for a few minutes, and then gently scrub his head with a soft-bristled baby brush.

Step 3: Shampoo. Wash the oil out of your baby's hair, using a mild baby shampoo, and while you're at it, give his head another gentle scrub with the baby brush or a clean washcloth.

More Timeless Tips

- If regular ol' baby shampoo doesn't do the trick, your doctor may suggest that you switch to an adult dandruff shampoo, like Head & Shoulders. Just be sure to get her permission first.

- Once the cradle cap goes away, you may return to washing your baby's hair every few days, rather than every day.

Belly Up

. . .

*"I saved your dried umbilical cords for a while, but then
I thought, Why on earth do I want these? To put in your prom corsage?
Eventually, I threw them away."*
—CLAIRE BRIED

HOW TO CARE FOR THE BELLY BUTTON

Step 1: Hail that little stump. That shriveled-up black remnant of the umbilical cord on your baby's belly is a reminder of how the two of you were once so intimately connected. Now, it sure is ugly, but it's also so completely and utterly beautiful.

Step 2: Dab your eyes. You probably started crying after you read Step 1, so take a moment for yourself here.

Step 3: Give it some room. Fold your baby's diaper down in the front, so it's not pressing on the cord or preventing air from circulating around it. And avoid putting anything on it, like alcohol. It doesn't speed the drying process whatsoever and, in fact, may irritate your baby's delicate skin.

Step 4: Wait. That's it. You're off the hook. Expect it to fall off after ten to fourteen days. If you celebrate your babe's one-month birthday, and the stump is still sticking around, consult your pediatrician.

More Timeless Tips

- Keep it dry. Stick with sponge baths until the cord falls off.

- Watch for infection. Call your doctor if you spot any redness, swelling, bleeding (more than a teeny, tiny bit), oozing, or PU stinking.

File Down

. . .

"We had special baby nail clippers, so no problem. Why was I not afraid
of these things? I don't know. I mean, I wasn't using hedge clippers or
anything. I'd just say, 'Oodgie coodgie, Mommy will fix this one.'
I just wasn't fearful."

—Sunchita Tyson

HOW TO CUT TINY FINGERNAILS

Step 1: Psych yourself up. Wielding sharp objects so close to
your little one's soft skin is scary stuff, but if you don't cut his nails
at least once a week, he'll scratch himself (and anyone else within
arm's length) to pieces and that would be so sad.

Step 2: Wait until he falls asleep. Only then will his hands be
relaxed, his fists unclenched, and his arms completely still.

Step 3: Take a deep breath. Or make that three. And do whatever you need to do to improve your vision: turn on a light, clean
your glasses, squint.

Step 4: Do the deed. Gently push the fingertip away from the nail and, using a baby nail clipper or baby scissors (ones with rounded points), trim the excess nail.

Step 5: File any rough edges. Sharp corners on the shortest of nails can still do damage, so round any jagged edges using a baby nail file.

Step 6: Exhale. Do a little dance. You did it!

More Timeless Tips

- Your baby's fingernails are fused to his fingertips for the first three to four weeks of life. Until then, skip the clippers or scissors and use a baby nail file to buff them back whenever necessary.

- If you do nick his fingertip, apply pressure with a sterile pad until the bleeding stops. Your baby will cry—and so may you!—but know that you'll both get over it. Once everybody calms down, go have a glass of wine and call a mom friend. You'll soon learn that drawing blood during a manicure can happen to even the best.

- Your baby's toenails are not only fused at first, but they're also super-flaky, meaning you couldn't clip 'em, even if you tried. So pressure's off, at least for a little while, on that end. Once you notice his big toenail growing regularly, give it a clip. As for the others? You probably won't have to worry about trimming them for months.

Cycle Gently

...

"I had a very, very small washer in my very, very small kitchen, and I'd wash every day at night, and that way it wouldn't mount up."
—SUNCHITA TYSON

HOW TO LAUNDER BABY CLOTHES

Step 1: Buy some special detergent. You don't need the super-expensive made-for-baby liquid soaps, but be safe and opt for a basic one that is free of dyes and perfumes. Those additives could irritate your little angel's delicate skin. If you don't miss the "fresh cotton" or "French lavender" scents, you can use it on your clothes, too. Simpler is better, no?

Step 2: Wash everything, especially hand-me-downs, before she wears it. That way, you'll be sure it's soft, clean, and non-irritating. Follow all the regular rules of laundry, too: Separate by color, and wash brights on cold and whites on warm or hot.

Step 3: Dry it. Hang it on the line and let your neighbors ooh and aah over just how tiny the clothes are, or pop them into the dryer, with no dryer sheets, obviously.

More Timeless Tips

• Get a jump-start on her laundry during the third trimester of your pregnancy, or you'll be frantically running loads while she's rolling around naked.

• Treat any stains before tossing the clothes in the wash. See page 144 for tips.

• Consider tossing her tiny socks in a mesh bag, or the washer monster may eat them up and you may never see them (or at least one of them) again.

• If you wash bibs with Velcro, fasten the ends together before popping them in the laundry. Otherwise, the Velcro will attach to every other item in your laundry and cause mayhem. OK, that's exaggerating a little. It'll cause a minor annoyance for whoever is doing the folding.

Clean Up
...

"I didn't know about Fels-Naptha when you were babies. So I'd scrub and scrub, but it never worked. You always wore onesies with cute appliqués—and huge carrot stains."

—Claire Bried

HOW TO REMOVE COMMON BABY STAINS

Step 1: Buy a bar of Fels-Naptha. It's a heavy-duty laundry soap that has been around for more than a hundred years, and it works like magic on just about every baby stain you can imagine.

Step 2: Treat the stain as soon as it happens. Undress your baby if he has pooped up his back, spit up, wet his onesie, dribbled breast milk or formula down his front, or flipped a spoonful of pureed peas onto his lap. (By the way, all these things are going to happen to you sooner or later —and sometimes all at once.) Just—ew!—try not to get any of it on you while you're doing it.

Step 3: Wash or scrape off as much of the stain as you can in cold water.

Step 4: Rub some Fels-Naptha on the affected area and then really work it into the garment. Let it sit for one minute.

Step 5: Rinse it with more cold water.

Step 6: Toss it in the washer and launder as usual.

More Timeless Tips

• Never throw a poopy onesie into your baby's hamper, even if it's 4 A.M. and you're totally exhausted. Walk it down the hall, put it in the sink, and at the very least, give it a good rinse in cold water, if not a good scrub with your super soap. Then make your way back to your bed. You'll be much happier in the morning.

Layer Up
· · ·

"I always dressed my babies in little white dresses and I'd take them for a buggy ride. It was a super-deluxe buggy."
—Betty Horton

HOW TO DRESS YOUR BABY

Step 1: Go for comfort over style. Newborn jeans and tiny dresses are absolutely adorable, but they're not as soft or supple as, say, a sweet cotton onesie. Always choose your baby's clothes with her happiness in mind.

Step 2: Look at yourself in the mirror. Take note of how many layers you're wearing.

Step 3: Dress your baby the same way, plus one more layer. So if you're wearing pants and a long-sleeved shirt, add a hoodie or sweater to your babe's ensemble. It's not that you're at all fat—you look like a model, really—but you do have a little more built-in, heat-preserving padding than she does.

More Timeless Tips

- It takes a while for your baby's internal thermostat to regulate itself, so if it's a real scorcher, either keep her inside until the mercury drops or dress her lightly, so she doesn't overheat. A short-sleeved cotton onesie, along with a wide-brimmed sun hat, will do. Also, try to keep her in the shade at all times. She can't wear sunscreen until her six-month birthday.

- Bring an extra blanket or jacket if you take her to the grocery store. It's always chilly in there.

- Don't leave your bundle bundled up once you bring her inside. Remove her jacket and any other extra layers, so she stays comfortable. If you notice that her forehead is wet with sweat, she's way too warm.

- Yo, those baby Bapes are fresh to death, for sure, but if she can't walk yet, she surely doesn't need shoes. Just keep her tootsies warm with socks.

6

Making

· · ·

A plastic, store-bought toy will never be a family heirloom, but anything you make will be treasured forever.

Put Your Stamp on It

· · ·

"We sent out birth announcements to our closest friends. I think it made my role as a mother more official. It had happened. It was done, and I was telling the world. Sending those announcements marked the beginning of a new life for my daughter and a new identity for me."
—RUTH ALSOP

HOW TO MAKE A BIRTH ANNOUNCEMENT

Step 1: Make your list. This is the moment you've been waiting for: your chance to introduce your little bundle of joy to the world. Decide with whom you'd like to share your happy news. Be sure to include all grandparents, aunts, and uncles (your own and your child's), close friends, and, if you'd like, also neighbors and colleagues.

Step 2: Choose a picture. Skip the one your sweetie took the very moment the baby exited your womb. That one's way too personal, and besides, you want to show your babe at her best, not her goopiest. Instead, stick with one where she looks happy and peaceful and, well, just like herself. Speaking of which, there's no need to plop her into some frilly dress or a Philadelphia Flyers sleeper for the shot. Allow her individuality to shine through, not yours.

Step 3: Choose your text. You'll need some sort of opener like "We're thrilled to introduce" or "Please say hello to," followed by your child's full name. Also include her weight, length, and date and time of birth. Finish with a closer like "With love and delight" or "Hugs and kisses," and your and your partner's names.

Step 4: Design it. Decide whether you'd like your announcement to be one-sided or two-; square, rectangular, or round; and in black-and-white or color. Then take it to a printer or, if you're computer savvy, log on to a custom stationery site, like tinyprints .com, snapfish.com, or shutterfly.com, choose a template, and drop in your image and text. Whatever service you use, don't forget to buy matching envelopes, too.

Step 5: Buy stamps. Go to the post office and pick out ones that match the tone of your announcement. Hint: This is not the time to use up those old Christmas, Hanukkah, or Kwanzaa stamps you bought last season. Go for the ones with flowers or hearts on them.

Step 6: Send 'em out. Sign them by hand, and if you like, add a personal note like "We can't wait for you to meet her!"

More Timeless Tips

- Buy at least ten more announcements than you think you need, so if you make a mistake, you have backup. Also, you can use the extras as thank-you cards to send to people who've sent you unexpected gifts.

- Make sure you buy the right stamps. Square cards cost more to send.

Top It Off

· · ·

"I always made things for my kids, but that's part of my gestalt, if you will. The night before Frank's bris, I decided to make him a little hat with some yarn I had in the basement. I made him his little kippah, and later both of his brothers wore it, too. Now, I have a shadow box frame with each of the boys wearing it."

—ESTHER SAFRAN FOER

HOW TO KNIT A HAT

Step 1: Gather your supplies. You'll need a set of size 10 (6mm) straight knitting needles, two big ol' blunt yarn needles (they look just like really fat sewing needles), and two balls of super-soft yarn, like Nature's Choice Organic Cotton. (If you're making the booties on page 155, use the same kind of yarn, so your set matches.)

Step 2: Get started. Cast on 64 stitches.

Step 3: Knit a rectangle. Use a garter stitch to knit 60 rows total. Somewhere in the middle of that, you'll run out of your first ball of yarn, so at the end of one row, work in your second ball of yarn, leaving both tails dangling.

Step 4: Cast off. Once you've hit your 60th row, loosely bind off your stitches. Before you snip your yarn, leave a very long tail, about 2 yards. You'll need it for Step 5.

Step 5: Sew up your hat. Fold your rectangle in half, length-wise, thread the tail of your yarn through your needle, and use it to sew both short ends of the rectangle together, from bottom to top. (That seam will be the back middle of your hat.) Next, you'll form a clover on top: Bring the front center of your hat to the back and sew together. Next, bring the center of each side to the middle and sew together. Finally, take your remaining yarn and weave the remaining teardrop-shaped holes closed, finishing with a knot at the center of the hat.

Step 6: Make pom-poms. Wrap some yarn around a 1-inch-wide piece of cardboard. The more you wrap, the fluffier the ball will be. Cut the yarn, ball-side, slide the tail through the loops and knot, leaving at least a three-inch tail. Slip out the cardboard, cut the loops, fluff, and trim. Use the tail to secure the pom-poms to the hat. Repeat twice more.

More Timeless Tips

- If the topper is too big for your toots, decrease the number of stitches you cast on (which form the circumference) as well as the number of rows you knit (which creates the height).

- You can find this pattern and others at lionbrand.com. For basic, step-by-step video knitting tutorials, visit learntoknit .lionbrand.com. Sometimes you've got to see it, not just read it, to really understand.

Toast Tootsies

. . .

"When I was on the subway, I always had something with me to knit for her. I just loved my daughter so much that I wanted to make things for her myself."

—RUTH ALSOP

HOW TO KNIT BOOTIES

Step 1: Gather your supplies. You'll need a set of size 8 (5mm) straight knitting needles, two big ol' blunt yarn needles (just super-fat sewing needles with eyes big enough to pass yarn through), and one ball of super-soft yarn, like Nature's Choice Organic Cotton.

Step 2: Get started. Cast on 24 stitches.

Step 3: Make the foot-part of the bootie. Do a simple garter stitch for 38 rows, 24 stitches a pop.

Step 4: Make the toe. On the 39th row, knit every two stitches together so you're left with 12 stitches. Then, knit the next row (all 12 stitches) same as always.

Step 5: Close the toe. Cut the yarn, leaving about a 15-inch tail. Thread it through your needle and dive it through your last 12 stitches. Pull the yarn to tighten the toe, cut, and knot off.

Step 6: Close the bootie top. Using the same needle, still threaded with your yarn, sew together the top of bootie from the toe toward the heel, leaving the last 2½ inches open for your baby's foot and ankle.

Step 7: Close the bootie back. Cut another length of yarn, about 15 inches long, and thread each end through a needle. Weave your needles back and forth through the stitches to create a heel, cut, and knot off.

Step 8: Add laces. Cut off an 18-inch piece of yarn, thread it through your needle, and weave it around the top of the bootie opening, so you're left with two laces dangling from either side of the front of the hole.

Step 9: Add tassels. You'll need four, two per bootie. To make 'em, wrap yarn around a 1-inch-wide strip of cardboard ten times. Cut a 4-inch piece of yarn, slip it between the yarn and cardboard on one side, and tie it as tight as you can. Then flip your cardboard over and cut through the yarn on the other side. Cut another 6-inch piece of yarn, wrap around the center of your tassel a few times, and knot it off, tucking any tail into the tassel. Tie the tassel to the laces and tie the laces into a bow.

More Timeless Tips

- If your booties aren't perfect, don't fret. Your baby won't even notice, and besides, the tiny imperfections, plus the love you put into knitting them, are what make them special.

- You'll know you've got the right-sized needles and yarn for this pattern if 36 rows of 17 stitches each makes a 4-inch square. If it takes you fewer stitches and rows to make a 4-inch square, use smaller needles. If it takes you more, use bigger ones.

- If your little one has even tinier feet, cast on 20 stitches and do 30 rows.

- Need a little technical help? Watch little videos on how to cast on and knit at learntoknit.lionbrand.com, and you'll be a pro in no time. You can find this pattern, and others, at lion brand.com, too.

Shoulder Up

. . .

"My teacher graduated me with a 100 in sewing.
I got a purple ribbon. I said, 'No one is that good.'
But I used to sew things for the girls. It was relaxing."

—BETTY HORTON

HOW TO SEW A BURP CLOTH

Step 1: Gather your supplies. You'll need a cloth diaper, about a quarter yard of colorful flannel (or any other soft, absorbent material), some straight pins, scissors, and a needle and thread.

Step 2: Match your layers. Lay your flannel, right side up, on a flat surface and lay your diaper on top of it, making sure your flannel is slightly larger than your diaper.

Step 3: Pin the edges, using a few straight pins. You want your layers to stay put while you sew.

Step 4: Sew together. By machine or by hand, stitch about a half inch in from the edge almost all the way around, stopping only a few inches short of closing your rectangle.

Step 5: Turn your masterpiece right side out. You can help it along, using the eraser side of a pencil.

Step 6: Sew the remaining hole closed. It'll just take a few more stitches.

Step 7: Quilt it. Stitch across the burp cloth a few times vertically, horizontally, or even diagonally. You'll use it to perform some heavy-duty tasks, like cleaning up spit-up and drool, and you'll wash it often, and the quilting just makes it a little sturdier.

More Timeless Tips

• You can also use a clean old pillowcase, trimmed to size, rather than a new piece of flannel or cloth diaper.

• If you're sewing by hand, use a simple (but strong) back stitch. Here's how: Double thread your needle and knot off the end. Then push your needle down through one side of the fabric and bring it back through the front a few millimeters ahead. Push your needle back down through your first hole and push it back through the front a few millimeters ahead of your second stitch. Press your needle down through your second stitch and back through the front a few millimeters ahead of your third, and repeat, leapfrogging your way along. Once you get to the end, make a couple of stitches in the same spot, pass your needle through the loop of thread, and snip.

Patch Together

. . .

"Both David and Rachel used this beautiful yellow blanket trimmed in satin that my husband's mother made. Rachel was very attached to it, so she used it on her bed as her blankie when she was a little older. I think we still have that blanket. We called it Yellow Blanket."

—Elaine Maddow

HOW TO MAKE A BABY QUILT

Step 1: Choose your fabrics, keeping baby in mind. You'll need two large square pieces, about one-and-a-quarter yards apiece. The material should be soft and washable. Think one side cotton, the other flannel. You'll also need a ball of heavy-duty crocheting yarn in a complementary color and just shy of one-and-a-quarter yards of batting, so your quilt is nice and fluffy.

Step 2: Stack everything. Put your bottom layer, right side down, on the bottom, followed by your batting, and then your top layer, right side up.

Step 3: Baste your fabrics. Put a safety pin (or curved quilting pin) in the very center and then keep pinning your fabrics together every six or so inches, working your way out on a diagonal to the corners. (By the time you're finished, your pins will form an x on your quilt.) These pins will simply hold your material together until you have a chance to sew it, so they don't have to be perfectly placed. Just be sure to smooth out your fabrics along the way to ensure a wrinkle-free blanket.

Step 4: Mark your ties. Those are the spots through which you'll thread and knot colorful pieces of yarn, which will hold the fabric together. (Tying the fabric together is quicker and easier than actually quilting the entire blanket.) Now just pin your fabric every four to six inches, starting from the center and forming a grid up, down, and across the blanket. To do so, just dip the pin through all three layers, down and up, nipping about a quarter inch of fabric in between.

Step 5: Tie one on. Double thread a needle with three to five yards of yarn (no knot at the end). Then, stitch horizontally across your quilt, using the pins you placed in Step 4 as your guide: Starting on top of the first pin and leaving a three-inch tail behind your first stitch, dive your needle down through all three layers of material, scoot it over a quarter inch and push it through the back and out the front again. Work your way across the row, repeating the stitch at every pin and removing the pins as you go. By the time you finish, it'll look like you have odd lines of yarn running across your quilt. Once you've got every mark stitched, use scissors to cut in between each, leaving two tails at each mark. Finally, tie each tail off with a square knot: Lay the right tail over the left and tie, and then lay the left tail over the right and tie. Trim the tails to your desired length.

Step 6: Bind the edges. Trim your batting by about a half inch all the way around. Next, fold the top and bottom layers of your fabric inward by a quarter inch, then pin and sew together. Or, to add a little more flair: Buy two-inch-wide double-fold bias tape or a two-inch-wide washable ribbon, fold it over the ends, and sew together.

Step 7: Give it to Baby. She'll cherish the quilt for her entire life, and depending on how well you sewed it, perhaps her own child will one day, too.

More Timeless Tips

- If you'd like, sign the quilt by stitching your initials and date in one corner, using embroidery floss.

- If you've got more time and want to go crazy, you can make a patchwork quilt. Rather than using two pieces of fabric, use as many pieces as you'd like, sewing four-inch (or so) squares together until they form your desired size. You can buy new fabrics, or make it a memory quilt by using fabrics from baby clothes, sheets, or blankets that your bundle no longer uses.

- If you're sewing your quilt by hand, use a back stitch. For a quick how-to, see More Timeless Tips from "How to Sew a Burp Cloth," page 159.

Soak It Up

. . .

"We made bibs out of sheeting or Turkish towels,
but you didn't have time to decorate them."

—Betty Horton

HOW TO MAKE A TOWEL BIB

Step 1: Choose a towel. Make it a clean, colorful and absorbent one.

Step 2: Make the neck hole. Fold the towel in half, short side to short side, and cut a half circle in the center of the seam. The circle should be large enough to comfortably fit around your baby's neck but not so big that all the pureed carrots he dribbles down his chin will land on his shirt. Four inches across, or the width of your favorite coffee mug, should be about right. Then, lift the top layer of fabric, and make a straight cut down from the circle to the short end of the towel.

Step 3: Finish the edges. Pin washable ribbon or double-fold bias tape along the straight unfinished edges leading to the neck hole, and sew it in place. Then, pin and sew a second piece of ribbon, or bias tape, around the neck hole, leaving eight to ten inches hanging off each end to form the ties; knot both ends.

Step 4: Give it a try. Tie it on your baby and feed him whatever food matches the color of your towel. You should be able to revel in your handiwork for at least one meal before it gets stained to pieces, right?

More Timeless Tips

- As your baby gets older (and taller), you can make longer bibs. Rather than folding the towel in half in Step 2, just fold the top edge down by a third.

- If your little monster doesn't sit still long enough to tie a bib on, then (a) you poor thing and (b) simply use one piece of ribbon or bias tape to finish all the edges and add a snap or two pieces of Velcro near the neck hole.

Go Bananas

· · ·

"Kids are so open, and there's beauty in their simplicity. They respond to things that are soft, that they can put in their mouths, that have faces. Toys require no complexity when they're that age. They don't need lights and music. It's all tactile."

—ERINN McGURN

HOW TO MAKE A SOCK MONKEY

Step 1: Choose a pair of socks. Make sure they're clean, colorful, and have no holes in the toes.

Step 2: Make the body and legs. Turn one sock inside out and lay it flat, so the heel of the sock, which will soon become the heinie of your monkey, is pointing upward toward the ceiling. Then draw a dotted line down the center of the sock, starting an inch or two below the heel and going to the sock's opening. Next, starting on the heel end, sew along both sides of that line, leaving about an inch in between the two seams. When you get to the opening at the end, sew off the ends, rounding them off slightly to make your monkey's feet. Finally, to free your monkey's legs, cut along the dotted line. Ah, he can run and jump now! Turn him right-side out and set him aside.

Step 3: Make his arms. Turn the second sock inside out and lay it on a flat surface in profile, so the toe is on the right, the heel is on the bottom, and the leg opening is on the left. Make one cut across the sock about two inches above the heel (on the leg-opening side). Then, cut that piece in half, lengthwise, to form your arms. Sew the rough edges together, rounding them off to a close at the cuff. Turn them right-side out and set aside.

Step 4: Make his tail. Take the remaining foot-side of the sock and cut it lengthwise. The top portion will become your monkey's swisher, so sew the rough edges, rounding it off to a close at the toe. Turn it right side out and set aside.

Step 5: Nab his kisser. Now, you've just got the bottom of your sock left. Carefully snip out the heel, leaving you with a pie-shaped piece of sock (when folded in half). Set it aside. Side note: Isn't pie just delicious? Maybe you should take a break right now and go have a piece. You know, just an idea.

Step 6: Make the ears. Out of the remaining foot portion of your sock, which should still be folded in half, snip out two half-moons. Sew them almost all the way closed, and then through that teeny tiny hole you left, turn them right side out again and set aside.

Step 7: Stuff his body. Press cotton batting or polyester fiber into your monkey through the hole in his crotch, using a chopstick, a pencil, or a knitting needle to get it into every nook and cranny. Fill him just enough so he's not too floppy and not too hard. Then sew up his hoo-ha by hand, running your stitch across the opening a few times so he's good and strong.

Step 8: Form his head. Wrap a piece of matching embroidery thread around his head several times, about 4 inches from the top, pull it tight, and knot it in the back, trimming off any excess.

Step 9: Connect his schnoz. Open up that heel piece you snipped in Step 5, and lay it horizontally across his face. You can turn the edges under for a neater look or leave them out for a sweetly tattered look. Then, sew almost all the way around it, leaving a tiny space to press in the filling. Finally, stuff the snout and sew it closed.

Step 10: Stuff the arms and tail. Using a chopstick, pencil, or knitting needle, push your fill all the way to the tips. Then sew the open ends closed.

Step 11: Attach the arms and tail. Press them against the body at your desired location, tuck the raw edges under, and sew them on.

Step 12: Attach the ears. Fold your ears in half and sew the raw edges together, so they look cupped like flower petals. Then sew them onto the sides of the head above the nose.

Step 13: Make the face. Using embroidery thread, make a few stitches across the snout to form a smile, a few on top to form nostrils, and a few on the front of the head (in line with the ears) to make eyes.

Step 14: Give the monkey to your baby, and watch him go bananas over it.

More Timeless Tips

• If your little one is well beyond the SOBE (sucking or biting everything) phase, feel free to use buttons for the eyes. Prior to that, though, it may be better to just embroider them with only thread, so there's no choking hazard.

• The classic sock monkey socks are Rockford Red Heels, but you can use any kind of sock you please.

Hop to It

· · ·

"If she falls, wait that split second. If her reaction is nothing, just say,
'Oopsie!' If she did hurt herself, scoop her up, fix it, and kiss it."

—CLAIRE BRIED

HOW TO MAKE A BOO-BOO BUNNY

Step 1: Gather your supplies. You'll need: one washcloth, a thin
ribbon (or a few thin ribbons), and a needle and thread.

Step 2: Lay your washcloth on a flat surface.

Step 3: Fold it in half diagonally. Bring the bottom right corner up to the top left corner to form a triangle.

Step 4: Roll it up. Starting at the upper left corner, roll your
washcloth as tightly as you can, so you finish with a long snake. If
you'd like to quit here, you can call it a boo-boo snake, but it'll be
good for nothing. Don't be lame. Keep going!

Step 5: Fold it in half. Bring both ends together so the washcloth forms a U-shape and wrap your fist around it in the middle.

Step 6: Fold the ears back. Take the two loose ends that are cur-
rently pointing up and fold them down toward you, so they meet

the bottom of the U. Now, you've got a bunny who is looking up at your ceiling.

Step 7: Make the head. Tie a ribbon, as tightly as you can, around the top third of your washcloth. Now you should be able to make out a bunny.

Step 8: Sew up any loose seams, using your needle and thread.

Step 9: Fluff up the ears. You want your bunny to look sharp when he goes about his business of making your baby feel better, right?

Step 10: Insert an ice cube. Whenever your little one gets a bump, nest an ice cube into the bunny's body and place it on the spot that hurts.

More Timeless Tips

• When your baby gets a little older, you can glue on googly eyes, a pom-pom nose, and a cotton tail. In the meantime, though, you'd better steer clear of small parts, which can present a choking hazard. There is no such thing as a Heimlich Hippo. If you must have a face, you can always sew one on with embroidery thread.

Milk It

. . .

"Neil was always putting things together. We had building blocks. They were cardboard. They looked like shoe boxes. We didn't have a lot of money, so we made sure that whatever we bought them would last and they'd learn from it."

—SUNCHITA TYSON

HOW TO MAKE HOMEMADE BLOCKS

Step 1: Drink milk. Or orange juice.

Step 2: Collect your empty quart and half-gallon cartons. Wash 'em first, of course.

Step 3: Cut the cartons. Measure up from the bottom 4 inches on a half gallon, or 2 ¾ inches on a quart, draw a line around the carton, and then, using a hefty pair of scissors, cut it. Save the bottom and recycle the top.

Step 4: Form the block. Take two bottoms of the same size and nest them together, so the bottoms are up on either end.

Step 5: Decide how crafty you want to be.
Not so crafty? Cover the block with adhesive contact paper, and voilà! You're finished!

Off-the-hook crafty? For every block, cut 6 squares of felt (either new or from old blankets or sweaters, first washed and dried at the hottest temperatures possible), measuring either 4 inches by 4 inches (for half-gallon blocks) or 2 ¾ inches by 2 ¾ inches (for quart blocks). Using embroidery thread, stitch them together to form a cube, and before you sew the final square, slip the milk carton block inside.

Step 6: Stack 'em with your baby and watch the thrill she gets when she knocks 'em down.

More Timeless Tips

- Add a jingle bell inside one, and your blocks will pull double duty as a rattle, too.

Spark Imagination

· · ·

HOW TO MAKE A SQUISHY CATERPILLAR

Step 1: Choose the body. Dig out an old pair of brightly colored (ahem, clean) stockings and snip off one leg about fifteen inches above the toe.

Step 2: Stuff it. For a squishy caterpillar, you can use cotton batting, polyester fiber, or even old nylons. For a noisy caterpillar, try six pieces of crumpled cellophane or wax paper.

Step 3: Knot off the end of the stocking and trim the excess.

Step 4: Cut five pieces of contrasting ribbon, in 8-inch lengths, and tie each segment around the stocking, between the balls of filling or paper. Secure each ribbon with a double knot.

Step 5: Name your bug-a-lug and present it to your baby.

More Timeless Tips

- This isn't, by any means, a fancy baby toy, but it doesn't have to be. To your little one, everything is new, and therefore stimulating. Besides, he'll learn so much more from you than anyone or anything else.

Shake It Up

· · ·

"You only need the basics. All those toys? Oh please. They're just material things. If babies are healthy and surrounded by love, that's all you need."

—SUNCHITA TYSON

HOW TO MAKE A ROLLING RATTLE

Step 1: Drink some coffee. It should be the kind that comes in a can, not a bag, but for your own sake, try to find a brand that's not totally cheap. You *know* those just give you a tummy ache. Once the can is empty, wash it out.

Step 2: Choose your noisemakers. Fill the can with anything you please, like dried beans, rice, pennies, or acorns.

Step 3: Secure the can's lid. Some heavy-duty tape, like duct tape, or even a few drops of Super Glue will keep it in place.

Step 4: Cover your can. The easy route: Wrap the canister in adhesive contact paper, making sure the ends are secure. The prettier route: Cut two felt circles, $4\frac{1}{4}$ inches in diameter, to cover the ends, and one felt rectangle, $5\frac{1}{2}$ inches tall and 13 inches wide, to cover the sides. Then, using embroidery thread, stitch the pieces together with the can inside.

Step 5: Set the rattle on the floor next to your babe. She'll love to push it around, especially if she can crawl behind it.

More Timeless Tips

- If she loves the can so much that she won't go anywhere without it, don't get mad because you bought this book. She's occupied, right? And happy, yes? So what if it's a little loud? At least you're not paying for batteries, too.

7

Relating

. . .

You have your own family now. Make it a priority.

Meet the Public

...

"I told people they had to call ahead of time. You want to enjoy their company and you want them to enjoy themselves, too, so I said, 'No pop-ins allowed!'"

—Sunchita Tyson

How to schedule visitors

Step 1: Make a plan with your partner, preferably before you go into labor. Of course, you're both excited to introduce your little bundle of joy to your families, friends, and the world, but you may differ on just how and when to do that. Some people want a few days or even weeks alone to spend getting acquainted with their baby and accustomed to being a new little family. Others prefer to have as many people in the delivery room as possible to greet their bundle the very moment he enters the world. Figure out what you both want and, most importantly, make sure that you agree to it.

Step 2: Release expectations. There's no doubt you are going to be more tired than you ever have been before in your entire life, so cut yourself some slack. You don't need to have home-baked goodies for every guest who strolls through your door. (They're there to see the baby, not eat.) You don't need to be up on the latest world events so you can make pithy conversation. Heck, you don't even need to get dressed up (or even dressed in the first place). After all,

you just pushed an entire person out of your hoo-ha (or had someone reach into your belly and *pull* her out), and your friends and
family need to understand that. Just brush your hair, pop a breath
mint, and if you want to really go crazy, slide into some non-
pajamas and put on a little lip gloss. Done. You're ready.

Step 3: Set dates and times. Abide by your schedule, and your
baby's, no one else's. Your mom may want to stay for the weekend, but if that stresses you out, invite her for an afternoon and
let her know you'd love her to stay longer once you get more settled. Your coworker may want to come over for lunch, but if that's
when the baby usually sleeps (and you, too), offer her another
time. Or, if you have a lingering guest, don't be shy about politely
showing her the door. Say something like, "I'm sorry, I'm so beat,
I think I have to take a nap now," or "Thank you so much for
coming over. You'll have to come again when I'm a little more
awake." She'll get the message.

More Timeless Tips

- There's no need to cram all the visits in within your baby's
  first week of life. Spread them out over the next few weeks,
  or even months, and know that with every day that passes,
  you'll only feel more energized and your baby will only get
  cuter. It may not seem possible right now, but it's true.

- Enlist your partner to help tidy up before guests arrive and
  make them comfortable once they do. Heck, if you're taking
  care of the baby full-time, enlist your partner to do *everything* for the next few weeks.

Build Trust

· · ·

"My father-in-law, who was Sicilian, came to the hospital, and while
holding Sal, opened a clove of garlic and cut it with a brand-new
pocketknife and then ate the garlic and then he breathed on Sal. Then he
closed the knife, handed it to me, and said, 'This is his knife from me.'
I was thinking, 'Are you crazy? You're breathing garlic on the baby!'
But it was a rite of passage."

—ROSEMARY GIUNTA

HOW TO INTRODUCE EXTENDED FAMILY

Step 1: Greet your relative with affection. Babies are highly
intuitive, and they notice when you're happy and open as much as
they notice when you're tense and trepidatious. Show your little
one that this person is special by offering a warm smile, hug, or
kiss. If you're delighted to see them, your baby will be more likely
to feel that way, too.

Step 2: Introduce them. If you want to get all proper, you should
technically address your relative first and say something like "Noni,
this is Eleanor." Then, tell your baby who she's meeting as well.
"Eleanor, this is Noni, your grandma. She came to see you!"

Step 3: Hand your baby off. You may only want to hold her
against your chest from now until, well, all of eternity, but think

about it, you also want her to have good, positive relationships with her extended family. The only way she can bond with them (and they with her) is if they get to spend time together and get to know one another. That's tough to do if you keep her too close.

Step 4: Give them space. Stand beside them for a while to make sure everyone is all right, but once your baby is settled and your relative looks comfortable, step back. If you hover too closely, your baby will always look at you and want you back. By allowing other people to love her and show her affection, you're teaching her that the world is a wonderful place full of wonderful people whom she can also trust.

More Timeless Tips

- Ask all of your guests to wash their hands before touching your baby, so they don't inadvertently spread any germs. Or make it even easier for them and keep a hand sanitizer nearby.

- If your baby starts to fuss, don't whisk her away immediately. Instead, give your relative a chance to calm her, or do your part by standing nearby and talking to and smiling at your baby.

- If your Uncle Joe's only move is to stiffly bounce the baby on his knee, and your baby is screaming accordingly, don't be afraid to pipe up with some tips like "Try rocking her. She loves that." You might feel awkward instructing an older relative, but Uncle Joe will thank you in the long run and, more important, so will your baby.

Tune Out

. . .

*"I listened to it, thanked 'em, and sorted out what I liked.
I lied a little bit, too, I suppose."*

—Betty Horton

How to deal with unwanted advice

Step 1: Listen. Be warned: Both baby bumps and babies are beacons for know-it-alls. Whatever you do, wherever you go, these advice-givers will find you and give you an earful. The good news is, every once in a while, they will have something useful to say. So, before you decide to tune them out, hear them out. You'll be able to tell within the first minute or so whether they'll be a resource or a nuisance.

Step 2: Thank them. You don't have to engage, debate, or ask follow-up questions. Instead, use the same tools you'd use if you saw a dear friend in an embarrassingly bad play, but rather than say, "Thanks for inviting me. That was some play! Very interesting," try "Thanks. I'll look into it," or "Thanks, that's good to know."

Step 3: Change the subject or, if you must, excuse yourself.

More Timeless Tips

- If someone is pressuring you, you can always use your pediatrician as backup. Say, "I see your point, I'll have to ask my pediatrician about that," or "I can see how that would be smart, but my pediatrician told me this way works, too."

- Ninety-nine percent of all unsolicited advice-givers only mean well, so try to keep that in mind, rather than take their meddling personally. Try to walk away from the conversation feeling loved, not insulted.

Show Gratitude

. . .

"If they thought enough of us to bring that little baby a gift, I'd certainly want to take time to acknowledge that. There's something special about them giving a gift, so there should be something special in return, too."

—Ruth Alsop

HOW TO WRITE A THANK-YOU CARD

Step 1: Stock up on cards and stamps. As a new parent, you'll be receiving more gifts than you could ever dream of, and each requires a thoughtful, handwritten thank-you in return.

Step 2: Choose your voice. You can either write the thank-you as yourself or, if you and your recipient share a great sense of humor, write it in your baby's voice.

Step 3: Address the recipient by name: "Dear Clementine."

Step 4: Offer thanks for the gift, and don't hem and haw. Begin the sentence with "Thank you for . . ." or "I'm so grateful for . . ."

Step 5: State, in simple terms, why the gift touched you. (If it's a present you haven't put to use yet, say what you plan to do with it in the future.) Try something like "The booties are so ador-

able, and I know they'll keep Baby's feet warm on chilly nights,"
or "The booties fit my feet perfectly, and even though I'm only
two weeks old, I can confidently say that they're just my style."

Step 6: Express your gratitude for the gift giver. After all, her
presence in your life is more important than her presents in your
life, right? Try something like "You're always so thoughtful" or
"I'm so grateful to have such a generous friend."

Step 7: Sign off. Try "With love," "Fondly," or "Warmly," and
then your name or Baby's name.

Step 8: Lick the envelope, address it, stamp it, and send it!

More Timeless Tips

• Keep it short. A few heartfelt sentences will do.

• Don't get all highfalutin with your language. Write how you
  speak; otherwise the receiver may suspect that the real you
  has been abducted by aliens.

• Be swift. The sooner you send your card, the more meaningful it will be. However, even if it takes you months to send it,
  still drop it in the mail. A very late thank-you is better than
  none at all. Besides, you've got a great (and most adorable)
  excuse.

Raise a Flag

. . .

"You need help. Everybody needs help, especially if you haven't done it before and you don't know exactly what to do. I didn't feel embarrassed at all by asking. I felt, why wouldn't I ask, if it helps me and my baby?"

—RUTH ALSOP

HOW TO ASK FOR HELP

Step 1: Speak up. Every new mom feels overwhelmed at some point, and more likely, at many, many, many points. So, if you're feeling like you can't keep your you-know-what together, don't suffer in silence. Instead, hold your head high, take a deep breath, and reach out to someone you trust. Opening up to your partner or a friend will make you feel supported and it'll make him or her feel valued. It's a win-win situation.

Step 2: Be specific about your needs. Do you require sympathy, guidance, or just someone to watch your baby for an hour so you can finally take a shower for the first time in two days? You'll be more likely to get what you need if you ask for it directly.

Step 3: Say thanks. Let your savior know you'll return the favor down the road.

Step 4: Feel proud. By seeking help, you've not only done yourself—and your baby—a favor, but you've also demonstrated tremendous resourcefulness and bravery. It sometimes takes guts to ask for help, and you have 'em. Pound your chest a few times, or pump your fist in the air. You rock!

More Timeless Tips

• If you're really struggling, know that you're not alone. In fact, 12 percent of women report being moderately depressed after giving birth, and another 6 percent report being severely depressed, according to the Centers for Disease Control. So, if you feel like you just can't get it together after a few weeks, seek professional help.

• Often, you won't even have to do the asking. After you bring your baby home, many of your friends will call or e-mail you to see if you need anything. They're not just saying that to be polite. They really mean it! So, for goodness' sake, tell them. Try something like "Right now, I'd kill for a tray of lasagna, and I know you make the best one in town." Who has time to cook with a newborn at home?

Draw Lines
...

"Be honest. Otherwise, you get resentful."
—Erinn McGurn

How to set boundaries

Step 1: Draw lines. Your extended family may have different ideas of not only how your relationship will be after the baby arrives but also how you should parent said baby. Suddenly, your mom starts dropping in uninvited every afternoon for a quick cuddle session, and your mother-in-law wages what seems to be a not-so-secret campaign urging you to feed your baby formula rather than breast milk. Talk to your partner about what is acceptable behavior and what isn't.

Step 2: Choose your messenger. Here's the rule: If it's your family who is overstepping, then you've got to be the one to buck up. If it's your sweetie's family, he or she has to take point.

Step 3: Present a united front. State your wishes and expectations in clear terms, beginning each sentence with either an "I" or a "We." Whatever you do, do not wimp out and use your honey as a scapegoat (e.g., "Of course you know, *I'm* fine with it, but Will isn't"). You will not only never forgive yourself, but you'll also hurt your own marriage over something totally stupid, and your family may hold a grudge against your sweetie, which will cause even more trouble down the road. Be sure to convey that it's nothing personal, but you're just trying to do what's best for your own family right now.

Step 4: Stick to your guns. You may be met with huffing or puffing or even anger, but they'll get over it, and you'll all be happier in the long run if you have an honest relationship.

More Timeless Tips

- This is standard parent-child and in-law–child crapola, so don't think you have it any worse than anyone else out there, even if you have to dog-ear this page and refer to it again and again. It's just part of this messy thing we call life.

- Your family and even some friends intrude because they care about you and your baby, and so remember that even the most annoying and offensive advice and behavior likely comes from a good place. There's love all around. Sometimes a little too much maybe, but that's a nice problem to have.

Time Share

. . .

"There comes a time when you want to establish your own holiday routines in your own house. When that time came for us, there wasn't any big to-do about it. We cut down our own tree and decorated the whole house. I had time to shop, because we weren't planning a big trip, and the kids opened their gifts on Christmas morning. We loved it!"

—Elaine Maddow

HOW TO HANDLE HOLIDAYS

Step 1: Decide what *you* want. Chances are, Grandma and Grandpa and Noni and Popi are all going to want to spend Baby's first Thanksgiving (and Baby's first Christmas, Baby's first Easter, Baby's first Memorial Day, Baby's first Labor Day, and oh, you get the point) with you. If your families don't live close by, or if they don't get along, or if you'd rather have a quiet day to yourselves so you can carve out your own family traditions, then you're going to have to make some tough decisions. Sit down with your partner, discuss your desires, and devise a plan together.

Step 2: Broadcast your plans. Unless your conversation starts with the lines "We'd love to spend the holiday with you! Your house or mine?" then be prepared to be met with resistance and disappointment, with, no doubt, a hefty side of guilt. Just remember, you're a grown-up now with your own family to look after, and you've got to make the best decisions for you, knowing that you can't please everyone all the time.

Step 3: Make alternative plans, if you'd like. Your baby does not know one day from the next, so reassure your relatives that if you celebrate the holiday with them a week early or late, it'll still be just as special. They just want to feel important and loved, and they want to be a part of your baby's life. Be thankful for that.

More Timeless Tips

- If you can't be with your relatives on a holiday, but you'd like to include them in the festivities, there's always Skype. A video call isn't exactly the same as being there in person, but it may satisfy the urge to interact with your baby and share in the day's celebrations. Or, at the very least, call on the phone. Send pictures. Do whatever you can to stay connected. Not only for your parents' sake but also for your baby's. You'll want him to know his family and feel surrounded by love.

Welcome Home

· · ·

"Sal was three when I had Mario. I'd gotten him a doll ahead of time, because I wanted to make sure he had an idea of what was coming. When I came home with Mario, he loved him. Mario was two and a half when I had Katie. He was running around the house in his cowboy boots and underwear, and he stared down at Katie in her bassinet, then looked at me, then back at her, and he said, 'Take her back.' I said, 'Honey, she's going to stay. This is her home.' It took him a little while to adjust."

—ROSEMARY GIUNTA

HOW TO INTRODUCE BABY TO AN OLDER SIBLING

Step 1: Let him know what's up before you bring the baby home. When he starts asking questions about your growing belly, sit him down and tell him the good news: He's going to have a baby brother or sister very soon. If he's too young to understand the concept, let the tone of your voice convey your excitement, and he'll likely go along. Also, read books about babies or visit friends with babies, so he can get an idea of what's ahead.

Step 2: Make change a positive thing. You'll have to reassure your not-as-little one that you love him to pieces, and you always will, even if you'll be pretty busy for a while tending to his younger sibling. If he has to vacate the nursery to make room for Baby, throw a "new room party," so his move down the hall feels like a celebration, not a displacement. Bring him to the hospital as soon as you can to meet the new addition. And consider getting him a little present to celebrate his new status as a big brother.

Step 3: Keep him involved. Let him feel a part of the excitement by allowing him to help pick out things like books, toys, and even room décor before the new baby arrives. Just don't allow him to pick out the name, unless, of course, you want a baby named Strawberry or Buzz Lightyear. And when Baby comes home, allow him to help out as much as he can or wants to, from keeping you company while you nurse to reading the baby a book.

More Timeless Tips

- Set aside time to spend with your older child each day. You can tell him you love him out the wazoo, but he needs focused, just-for-him time to actually see it and feel it.

- If your older child starts acting like a baby to get a little more attention, he's sending the message to you that he needs some more lovin'. Give him a few extra hugs and kisses, ignore his regressions, and cheer him on when he behaves well.

8

Surviving

. . .

You already got through the childbirth.
You can do anything, Mama.

Rest Up

. . .

"I remember being so tired. One night, I heard Rachel crying and I got up in a daze and walked into the closet to get a bottle! The fatigue is something I won't forget. You feel like it'll never end, but we all made it through and you will, too."

—ELAINE MADDOW

HOW TO COMBAT EXHAUSTION

Step 1: Be flexible. *Everybody* will tell you, "Just nap when the baby naps," which seems like good advice, especially considering that newborns snooze for about sixteen hours every day. So if you can do that, good for you. If you can't, or you'd rather spend that time eating a meal, taking a shower, or doing laundry, that's OK, too. Listen to your body, and do whatever you need to do at any given moment. Remember, the bar is set pretty low here. Your only job is to care for the baby when she needs it. That means everything else, from getting dressed to combing your hair, is purely optional.

Step 2: Accept help. If you are lucky enough to have a partner who can take over some early mornings or even nights, let your partner do it. If you are formula feeding, this will be easy, and if you are breast-feeding and can pump a bottle or two ahead, it's doable. (Just remember, you still need to pump every time the baby eats, to keep your supply steady. The benefit: Pumping is often quicker than nursing, so you might be able to catch a few more winks this way.)

Step 3: Get some fresh air. The idea of staying inside all day, watching *Law & Order* reruns, while your baby nurses and naps, seems kind of luxurious, and it is for a while, but after a few episodes, the stale air coupled with the repeated "dom-dom" sound after every scene will only amplify your exhaustion. If it's nice outside, pull yourself together, get dressed, put the baby in a carrier or stroller, and take a walk. Chances are, your baby will enjoy the ride (and fall asleep), and you'll feel refreshed by the change of scenery and the exercise.

Step 4: Enjoy it. If ever there were a time to revel in your zombie state, now is it. Every new parent is exhausted, and for good reason. Take a look at that little peanut in her crib. She's worth every sleepless moment. And even though you may not believe it now, within three months, you'll all be sleeping for five hours solid at night, and in six months, you may even have your long, dreamy nights back. This time is so short. Treasure it.

More Timeless Tips

- If you ever get into a betting situation with your partner, wager a night of sleep with earplugs. For the first year, even when your baby is zonked, you'll have a tendency to sleep with one eye open, just to make sure she's fine. If you can spend one night with earplugs every so often, allowing your partner to take the night shift, you'll wake up more refreshed than you ever knew possible.

- If you're feeling particularly lousy about yourself, if you haven't shaved your legs in weeks, and if you don't even remember what it was like to do your hair, heed Grandma's advice: Put on a little lipstick, and you'll be fine. (Well, maybe not FINE-fine, but it only takes a second, and you'll feel a little better.)

Stay Solid

...

"We didn't have 'date nights,' because we always had a good time together. When the kids were sleeping, we'd have candlelight dinners."
—SUNCHITA TYSON

HOW TO KEEP YOUR RELATIONSHIP WITH YOUR PARTNER HEALTHY

Step 1: Remember yourself. Everyone knows the first step in loving anyone else is loving yourself, right? And that might be hard if you've been wearing the same tank top with spit-up on the right boob for a week. So, if you can find a moment, take a shower, brush your hair, look at yourself in the mirror (in flattering light, of course). Remember your body. You've been sharing it with someone else (and you might still be), but you are still you. And now you're a sexy mama, too. Rejoice in it.

Step 2: Talk to each other. Preferably about something other than poop.

Step 3: Create space. You will be spending a ton of time at home together looking after the little one, but it will probably feel like you're tag teaming the tiniest wrestler ("I have him. You get the diaper! Hurry!!!") rather than spending quality alone time. Those long days (and longer nights) of staring deep into each other's eyes are gone for now. So instead, make time for each other. After the baby goes to bed, share a nice dinner (even if you have to have it delivered) and gaze at your beloved over candlelight. Or, if you can swing it, hire a sitter, enlist your mother-in-law, or have a friend come over for a few hours, and have a night on the town. Just remember, try to talk about something other than poop.

More Timeless Tips

- You might not have the desire, or the means, to go out together very often. That's OK. You are sharing this new wonderful thing together that, in itself, is an adventure. Just make the little things count. Say "I love you," even when you're tired. Share a quick smooch as you're handing over the baby. And step back, every now and again, between sleepless nights and crying jags (yours and the baby's), and remember that that person right there, talking about poop, that's the person you fell in love with.

Get Grounded

...

"When Ronnie was born, he didn't look very good. I swear to God, he looked like a monkey. And his head came to a point! But you know what? I loved him anyway."

—MARY HUFF

HOW TO HANDLE YOUR EXPECTATIONS

Step 1: Celebrate your delivery. You'd planned to have a natural water birth in a holy pool surrounded by chanting faeries, but Mother Nature had something else in mind? That's OK. The way you gave birth—with drugs or without, vaginally or via cesarean, in two hours or forty-two hours, in a taxicab or in a birthing center—doesn't reflect upon who you are as a woman, or how you'll be as a mother. Even if your delivery wasn't how you'd expected, focus on what you got out of it: a beautiful, bouncing baby.

Step 2: Redefine cute. You might not have envisioned having a baby with a conical head, blotchy skin, a hairy back, and more wrinkles than you, but chances are, your little cherub may have one (or all) of those features when he's just arrived. And in that moment, you will suddenly realize that hairy, wrinkly, splotchy cone heads are just about the cutest things on the face of this planet. Take plenty of pictures. You'll be amazed how quickly babies change, and when his skin fills out, his head rounds out, and his smile spreads across his face, you'll look back so fondly at these first snaps of your little old man.

Step 3: Be patient. No matter what you've read or heard, your baby likely won't nap at 9 A.M., noon, and 3 P.M. every day and begin sleeping through the night after a month. You aren't some sort of epic failure if he misses a nap or it takes him a little longer to get the hang of this whole sleeping thing. All babies need to learn how to put themselves to sleep, and they all do it at different times, but remember this: Eventually, every baby, even yours, will sleep through the night.

Step 4: Cut yourself some slack. If you can't breast-feed or, for whatever reason, don't want to, use formula. If you don't have time or energy to make homemade baby food, buy it. The important thing is that your baby is getting all the nutrients he needs, served up by a caring and (relatively) calm mom. However you feed your tiny one, enjoy it. This is the only time you'll have such closeness. Soon enough he'll be asking for money to order pizza with his friends.

More Timeless Tips

- If you find yourselves surrounded by friends and family who begin every other sentence with a disapproving "Well, when my firstborn was three months, he'd already . . . ," tune them out entirely. (See page 206 about how to find support.)

Reach Out

· · ·

"So much of parenting is about the support networks that you have.
As they say, it's not one hand clapping."

—ESTHER SAFRAN FOER

HOW TO GET THE SUPPORT YOU NEED

Step 1: Take classes. Your pediatrician's office, local hospital, or birthing center probably offers classes in childbirth, child care, and breast-feeding. Take advantage of them. You'll likely learn more practical tips from the childbirth educators, midwives, doulas, and lactation consultants explaining things live, in person, than you will learn anywhere else (except, of course, in this book). And you'll be able to ask all the questions that have been keeping you up at night. Plus, you'll meet other mothers and couples who are going through exactly what you are going through, right now. You might be bored for part of it, but you'll realize that you aren't at all alone.

Step 2: Reconnect with old friends. You remember those high school and college friends who disappeared while you were working sixty-hour weeks, flying to Paris, and dancing on tables? Well, they were home, raising kids. They have a jump on you, and maybe because of that, they'll be eager to offer you support, encouragement, and advice. Find them and say, "Hi, Mama!"

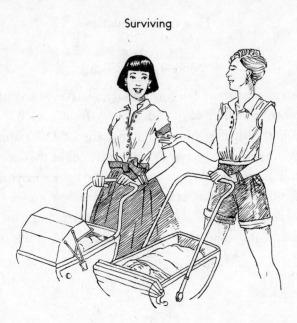

Step 3: Be a joiner. There may be local moms' groups in your area, catering to almost any demographic. (Knitting mom? You're in luck. Yoga mom? Come on down. Harley mama? Vroom-vroom.) Even if you aren't a joiner, find the group for you and your little one and go, at least once. You might even meet a few people you like.

Step 4: Go online. Whatever social media service you feel comfortable using, you can find other moms like you, usually with just a quick search. For example, there's a hashtag on Twitter, #bfcafe, which breast-feeding moms use to find one another, chat, and trade tips. Even if you're getting anonymous advice from someone who goes by BAB3MAMA! or MOMISMURF, you'll connect enough to realize that you aren't alone.

More Timeless Tips

- It's a total bummer, but don't be surprised if your single friends without children start to drift away from you. You are all about the babies right now, and they are not. Don't worry, you haven't lost them forever, but they may not be the ones to talk about morning sickness with. And, who knows, maybe they'll be calling you in a year or two, after they've grown tired of working sixty-hour weeks, flying to Paris, and dancing on tables. And, wonderfully, you'll be able to help guide the way.

Cheer Up

...

"I think I had some blues, but we didn't talk about it a lot. It would've helped me if I'd talked about it, but my husband didn't want me to feel bad. I had to fight back. I just kept going and going. I swung with it. You adjust or you go for help."

—RUTH ALSOP

HOW TO GET HELP IF YOU HAVE
POSTPARTUM DEPRESSION

Step 1: Understand what's normal. After the fairy dust settles and all the relatives go home, you're left at home, often alone, with a baby. And, no matter what the TV says, it's not all lovely, wonderful bliss. You're tired. You hardly have time to eat right. Your hormones have bottomed out. As a result, you could experience the baby blues, which means that for a couple of weeks, you might feel moody, sleepless, ravenous (or not at all hungry), a bit flighty, a little weepy, and sometimes just really bitchy. Don't worry, it's all par for the course. After a little shut-eye, a decent meal, and a chance to adjust, you'll be back to yourself in no time. If not, proceed to Step 2.

Step 2: Check yourself. If your symptoms feel a little more dire or they don't let up after two weeks, you could have postpartum depression. Step back, if you can, and assess how you're feeling and behaving. If you burst into tears at 3 A.M. because your neighbor's dog just woke up your baby *again*, that's probably just the baby blues. If you're crying all day for no apparent reason, that sounds like PPD. If you sneak a second bowl of ice cream after the baby falls asleep? Baby blues. If you sneak an extra half gallon? It could be PPD. If you're worried that you haven't been on a date in a month, and even if you did have time to go on one, all of your clothes are covered in spit-up and your hair is a mess? Baby blues. If you don't even care about going on a date, or about your partner, or your baby, or really anything at all, you definitely have PPD. Proceed to Step 3.

Step 3: Get help quick. The good news about PPD is that it's totally treatable. Talk to your doctor and ask for help. Otherwise, your symptoms may hang around for a year or longer and nobody, including you and your baby, deserves that. Your doc will likely hook you up with a therapist and maybe even a prescription, and you'll be loving your life, yourself, your sweetie, and your baby again in no time.

More Timeless Tips

- Postpartum depression is more common than you think. In fact, up to 18 percent of all women report having depressive symptoms after giving birth, according to the Centers for Disease Control. Still, even if it was the rarest illness on the planet, who cares? There is no such thing as "supermom." Don't be ashamed, ever, about your feelings, and don't be afraid to ask for help.

- Whether you've got the blues or depression, there are things you can do to help yourself: try to relax, get outside every day, eat as healthy as you can, and stay connected to your friends and loved ones. Always remember that you are not alone.

Space Out

. . .

"No matter how busy you are, you need to set aside some time for yourself. I'd go and get my hair done, because it made me feel relaxed and beautiful."

—Christine Samuel

HOW TO MAKE TIME FOR YOURSELF

Step 1: Give yourself permission. Just because you have a baby at home doesn't mean that doing something by yourself or going somewhere alone for a few minutes or hours makes you a horrible mother. On the contrary, if you get some fresh air and do something to invigorate yourself, you'll come back happier and better equipped to share that joy with your little pip.

Step 2: Enlist help. Ask your partner, mother, friend, or a babysitter to watch the baby for a few hours. Obviously, the world will probably keep spinning if you don't get a haircut for a year, but why test it?

Step 3: Make the most of it. If you can find a free hour, don't waste it sitting on the couch eating Triscuits and watching Bravo, unless, of course, that's what you want to do more than anything else in this world, and really, who could blame you? But if you fritter away your free time, you'll be back on baby duty before

you know it and you'll feel like you didn't really get to do anything.

More Timeless Tips

- Have a plan in place, so you're ready to go when you have a
  free moment. Some ideas: Go to the coffee shop, order a ri-
  diculously expensive frozen beverage with whipped cream, and
  tell the barista your name is "Gigi." Go to the nail salon and
  get your toes painted fire-engine red. Meet your best bud at
  the park and jog (or OK, walk) a lap. Catch a movie matinee
  and don't forget the popcorn and Milk Duds.

Go Out

. . .

"I had great people. It was critical. My first babysitter was a certified English nanny. Who else would be good enough to take care of my first child? She wasn't exactly Mary Poppins, but she actually had a certificate from nanny school in England."

—ESTHER SAFRAN FOER

HOW TO FIND A GOOD BABYSITTER

Step 1: Get references. If your super-picky neighbor perfectionist friend finds a particular sitter up to snuff, your vetting process will be much easier. So ask your friends and neighbors first. If that doesn't work, put the word out that you're looking for someone in your various networks, like your church, bowling league, or radical knitters group. Still no luck? Go online and try neighborhood message boards or even sitter services, like sittercity.com.

Step 2: Set up an interview. Once you find one or preferably several candidates, invite each one over for a question and answer session. Ask about people's previous experience and qualifications, what they like about working with kids, whether they know CPR or first aid, where they live, and also their hourly rate. Also, perhaps most important, ask them for the names and numbers of three other families they've worked for, and let them know you'll be calling those families.

Step 3: Check their references. You want to find a babysitter who was beloved by her former charges and employers, so call every reference and have a good chat.

Step 4: Set a trial run. Once you've found a sitter you like and feel good about on a gut level, set a date to have her watch the baby while you are still at home. That way, you can see the way she interacts with your child and also how your baby responds to her. After you feel comfortable, set another trial run, where you pop in and out of the house during that time. Grab a quick lunch at the end of the block and then come home and check in. Pick up your dry cleaning and come home. You'll have a chance to see your sitter in action, and once you feel comfortable, you'll be able to confidently leave for longer periods.

More Timeless Tips

- If you've never been the "boss," it might feel a little awkward to tell the sitter what to do. But chances are, she'll appreciate the direction. After all, it's much easier for her if she knows what's expected of her, than if she has to try to guess.

- If you're not yet ready to leave your tiny bundle with a sitter, consider hiring a "mother's helper," basically a sitter-lite, who watches the baby while you stay home and do whatever else you need to do, like wash your hair, pay bills, or even just read a book. It'll give you a much-needed break without costing you any peace of mind.

Reclaim Yourself

. . .

"I gained thirty pounds, but I'm only five-one, so that was 25 percent of my body weight! I breast-fed like a maniac, so I lost twenty-two pounds in the first three months. Then it took me a year to lose those last eight pounds. I worked out. I ate healthy. I took walks with the kids, and I'd use them as little weights for fun."

—Erinn McGurn

How to lose the baby weight

Step 1: Revel in the progress you've made already. Just by giving birth, you've lost double digits. Between your baby, the placenta, and the amniotic fluid, we're probably talking around twelve pounds. Depending on how you look at it, that might be the hardest, or easiest, twelve pounds you've ever lost!

Step 2: Breast-feed if you can and want to, and you'll burn up to five hundred calories a day and lose a pound a week, without even breaking a sweat.

Step 3: Get moving. Once you're home from the hospital and you feel up to it, you can start stretching. You haven't been able to touch your toes for months, so make sure you've still got the moves. When you're feeling a little bolder, push your little one around the block in his stroller, and work your way up to longer and longer distances every day. About six weeks after you've given birth vaginally, or eight weeks after a cesarean, you can resume your regularly scheduled workouts. If you can't remember what yours were, try doing thirty minutes of intervals (alternating hard bouts of the cardio of your choice with easy bouts) a few days a week. Also, add twenty minutes of strength training twice a week. And yes, repeatedly lifting your baby over your head definitely counts as strength training.

Step 4: Eat well. If you went a bit off the rails with your food choices during your pregnancy, now is the time to bring back good habits. After all, you need all the energy you can get to keep you going throughout the day (and night), and if you're breast-feeding, you also need several hundred extra calories a day to ensure steady milk production. At every meal, make half your plate fruits and veggies, have a little lean protein, eat whole grains, and try for a serving of fat-free or low-fat dairy.

More Timeless Tips

- Be patient. It took you nine months to put the weight on, and it'll likely take you nine months to take it all off.

- Don't forget about your hoo-hoo. You probably did Kegels out the wazoo while you were pregnant to prepare for delivery, and you should keep doing them now to help you restore everything down below. Work up to twenty-five a day at ten seconds per squeeze, so when you have the time and energy to have sex again, you'll be ready to go-oh-oh! Also, you know how you just peed a little when you laughed? These exercises will help put a stop to that.

Suit Up

• • •

*"Going back to work made me a better mom, because
I was happier. I felt balanced, and I think my kids felt balanced, too.
You don't want your kids to be the only thing that fulfills you.
That's a lot of pressure on a kid."*

—CLAIRE BRIED

HOW TO GO BACK TO WORK

Step 1: Make a plan. Though the sleepless nights may seem endless, your maternity leave will fly by. So, whether you plan to hire a babysitter, tag team with your partner, enlist your mother, or drop your bundle at day care, it's best to have your child-care plan in place as soon as possible. This will make the transition back to work easier when the time comes.

Step 2: Adjust your mind-set. You probably won't be terribly excited to go from basking in the glow of your beautiful baby to basking in the glow of your cubicle's fluorescent lights, so steel yourself and try to remember that while you've created this beautiful thing at home, you've also probably created some pretty amazing things at work, too. Focus on what you love about your job, remind yourself of how good you are at it, and if you need extra inspiration, make a list of new work-related goals. Just because your baby is growing doesn't mean you stop. Of course, there's also a chance that you're champing at the bit to get back to work, and if that's the case, go, you!

Step 3: Dress up. You may not be able to rock your pre-baby work clothes for a little while yet, so invest in a few new outfits that will carry you through this transition. You'll feel back in the groove when you're out of your sweats and in sharp new duds.

Step 4: Find your focus. Nine to five may seem like forever, so remember why it is you're there. Keep a photo of your baby in your work area, call and check in at home occasionally, and don't be afraid to talk to the other moms at work. You can't be in two places at once, but you don't have to pretend that you never had a baby, either. You may find that you can focus on your work even better when you remember what it is you are working for.

More Timeless Tips

- If you plan to continue breast-feeding, the most recent federal laws require employers to provide time and space to pump. Talk with your boss and, if need be, check your legal rights, to make sure you are given what is required for you to care for your baby.

- Get rid of the guilt. You're doing what you have to (or simply want to) do for yourself, your baby, and your family. You're allowed. Work it, Mama.

9

Enjoying

· · ·

Parenting is not all fun and games, but the more you make it so, the happier everyone will be.

Be Prepared

· · ·

*"Don't take so much gear that you don't want to go.
It's important that you go places. Ask yourself, Do I really need all that
stuff just to go to the grocery store? On short outings, just bring a diaper
and a bottle. What more do you need?"*

—ELAINE MADDOW

HOW TO PACK A DIAPER BAG

Step 1: Load it with the basics for a quick diaper change:

• Diapers: Never leave home without at least three, and
pack more if you're going to be away for more than a few
hours.

• A changing mat: Some diaper bags come with one, and if
you've ever seen some of those plastic changing stations in
grocery stores, or worse, gas stations, then you already
know how happy you'll be to have it.

• Wipes: Bring a good stack in an airtight container.

• Petroleum jelly or diaper-rash cream: The jelly helps
prevent rashes and the cream helps heal them.

• A plastic bag: Or two. If there's no trash can near, you don't
want to be walking around with a poopy diaper loose in
your bag.

Step 2: Prepare for accidents. In case of diaper leakage, spitting up, changes in weather, and any other unforeseen events, stash:

- An extra outfit or two for your baby: You *will* need them. Just make sure they're weather-appropriate and the right size.

- An extra pair of socks: It might get chilly, or more likely, he might lose one along the way.

- A blanket: If it gets cold or windy, you'll be ready.

- A swaddling blanket: If the sun shines too brightly, you can drape this breathable fabric over your baby's exposed parts or even over the entire stroller.

- A burp cloth: Don't forget one, unless you feel like lugging around an extra outfit for yourself, too.

Step 3: Bring nom-noms. If you're going to be gone over mealtime (and even if you're not), it's always good to be ready with some nosh:

- A bottle: Fill it with breast milk, or bring your formula fixin's in case he gets hungry and you don't want to, or can't, nurse.

- Baby food: If you bring a jar, don't forget the spoon. If you're bringing finger food, store it in an airtight container.

- A bib.

- Snacks for you: You can surely work up an appetite or a thirst when you're lugging all of this gear.

Step 4: Bring your own entertainment:

- A pacifier: Or two, in case he drops one.

- A toy: If it comes on a ring, you can hang it on the outside of your bag.

- A book: Opt for small and sturdy board books like *Baby Touch and Feel: Animals*, rather than, say, your *Complete Calvin and Hobbes*, which weighs more than twenty-two pounds.

Step 5: Don't forget your own stuff. Why bring your purse when you're already carrying one ginormous bag? Tuck your wallet, cell phone, and lip gloss in an outer pocket and you're good to go!

More Timeless Tips

- Luckily, you'll only have to pack your diaper bag once. After that, you simply have to restock it whenever necessary.

- If you hang your diaper bag off your stroller handlebars, make sure it's light enough so it doesn't tip your stroller when you walk away.

- Follow the same rules in choosing a diaper bag as you would a carpet. Dark or patterned ones will hide stains better than light-colored or plain ones. Also, you're going to have to look at the thing every single day for the next couple of years, so buy one you won't get tired of.

Hit the Road

· · ·

"Get them familiar with their car seats first. They have to like being in their seats. Otherwise, they'll drive you bananas."
—ERINN MCGURN

HOW TO SURVIVE A CAR RIDE

Step 1: Be safe. Roughly 84 percent of all infant car seats are installed wrong, so after you put yours in (and preferably before you bring Baby home from the hospital), get it checked by a certified safety technician. (Find one near you at seatcheck.org.) By the way, the rear middle seat is the safest spot, followed by the one behind the passenger seat.

Step 2: Pack up. In addition to her diaper bag, make sure you bring some books and toys, and keep them in an accessible location. Also, keep a bottle at the ready so, if you're not driving, you can sit in the back and feed her without pulling over (or at least keep her happy until you can).

Step 3: Keep the adjacent seat clear. You've probably spotted other parents sitting in the backseat with their babies and subsequently vowed to never be That Mom. In your car, it would be adults up front, kids in the back, right? Well, you may soon learn that it's less fun to sit up front and attempt a conversation when your squirt is two feet behind you screaming her head off. Not that you should start out in the backseat next to her, but it's always nice to have that option if necessary.

Step 4: Time your departure. If she likes to sleep in her car seat, make the most of her naptime and leave right before she nods off. That way, you'll at least be able to start your journey in peace and she'll get an hour or two of solid snoozing.

Step 5: Pull over whenever necessary. Gone are the days when you could do that 240-mile drive in three and a half hours flat. Now you must abide by a few new rules of the road, which are: (1) As soon as you get on the highway, she'll poop so much, it'll squirt out of her diaper and go up her back; (2) as soon as you hit traffic, she'll get very, very hungry; and (3) minutes before you arrive at your destination, she'll fall sound asleep. Since it's never safe to take her out of her seat while you're on the road (even if you're at a standstill), always take the first exit, find a safe place to park, and do what you need to do. You will become intimately acquainted with every rest stop, scenic lookout, and roadside fast-food joint between your house and your parents' house, your in-laws' house, and wherever you go on vacation. Allow extra time for your journey and just try to enjoy it.

More Timeless Tips

- Those roll-down sunshades, which attach to her window, may seem like a good idea, but if you're in an accident, they turn into dangerous projectiles. Don't use them.

- Make a playlist of your baby's favorite songs for your trip. If she gets upset, try pumping up the jam.

- If it's just the two of you in the car, talk or sing to her from the front seat so she knows you're near.

- Never try to lean back and peek at her while you're driving, or you could swerve off the road or, worse, crash. If you really need to lay your eyes on her, pull over.

- Some hospitals offer free classes to teach you how to safely strap your baby into her car seat. If yours does, take it.

- Gas up before you go. The lull of the engine puts many babies to sleep, and if she does nod off and you have to pull off to fill your tank, chances are she'll wake up.

Play It Out

. . .

"Even when they're little, give them a pot and a wooden spoon and they'll smack it. An empty box? That's a toy. When I was little, I remember making mud pies in the garden. Turn your kids loose, give them space and opportunity to use their imaginations."

—Claire Bried

HOW TO ENCOURAGE IMAGINATION

Step 1: Make conversation. Sounds like a no-brainer, but it must be said. Ask your baby questions and wait for her answer, even before she can talk. She hears you. The more you interact with your baby, the quicker she'll learn and the more creative she'll become. For example, if you give your love bug a toy car and lay her on the floor, she might try to eat it. But if you show her how it goes and you make zooming noises to go along with it, well, depending on how old she is, she'll still probably just try to eat it, but eventually she'll also try to drive it.

Step 2: Make believe. When you're bouncing her on your knee, ask her how fast the horsey goes. When you're rocking her to sleep, sing her the song about the baby in the treetops. When you're feeding her pureed pears, pretend the spoon is an airplane and her mouth is the landing strip.

Step 3: Make music. Give her some pots and pans, show her how to pat the couch cushions, give her a toy piano, which she can bang on or kick. All that noise is music to her ears.

More Timeless Tips

- Give her time, and space, to get a little messy. If you're always keeping her occupied or cleaning up after her, she'll never have the freedom to let her mind roam.

- When buying toys, go for ones that encourage creativity and interactivity, like a set of wooden blocks or a box of crayons, not ones that just occupy or entertain her.

- Set an example for her. Draw, paint, sing, dance like a maniac, and tell her made-up stories, and she will follow suit.

Make Sweet Dreams

· · ·

"I'd read to the kids, but they liked to have their father read to them. Ty would start reading and the next thing you'd know, he'd drift off and the kids would laugh and climb on him."

—Sunchita Tyson

HOW TO READ A BEDTIME STORY

Step 1: Choose a book. Go for one with bright colors and, at least in the beginning, few words. Unless your baby is a genius and can actually follow a story line, the plot matters less than the sound of your voice, the pictures, page turns, and, most of all, the time spent together.

Step 2: Get cozy. Turn off all distractions, like the radio or television, dim the lights a bit (but not so dark as to strain your eyes), and cradle your baby, already bathed, dressed, and fed, in your arms or on your lap.

Step 3: Put some heart into it. Position the book so your little one can see the pictures, and begin reading aloud slowly, using different voices and intonations.

Step 4: Kiss your babe good night after you finish the book. Swaddle him, if necessary; tell him you love him; turn off the lights and—at last!—go plop on the couch with a glass of wine. You deserve it!

More Timeless Tips

• Reading to your baby will make her smarter, so do it as often as you can. It doesn't have to be a children's book, either. As long as you read with feeling, she'll be captivated by the newspaper ("The Supreme Court ruled unanimously in the vote for . . ."), a cookbook ("Preheat the oven to 350 degrees . . ."), the *Onion* ("Prick Veterinarian Keeps Dachshund Waiting in Empty Lobby for 45 Minutes"), or even an issue of *US Weekly* ("Miss USA is dating one hot Canadian!").

• As your baby gets older and develops preferences, allow him to choose his favorite book. If he's having trouble deciding, give him a choice between two. And ask questions throughout the story, preferably ones that don't have right or wrong answers. For example: "What would you do?" "What do you think happens next?" "Do you have any friends like that?" Make it an interactive experience, not a quiz.

- Stick with the same book a few nights in a row; it'll help your child develop his language skills more quickly.

- Join your local library. It's free!

Coochie Coo

. . .

"I talked in baby talk to my kids, but they were probably thinking, C'mon, Mom, talk right. Don't talk so silly. I think it's good, but sometimes it gets a little stupid, too. I'm not sure where the line is between good and stupid, but you'll sure know when you cross it."

—MARY HUFF

HOW TO TALK TO YOUR BABY

Step 1: Become a chatterbox. The more you talk to your baby, the smarter she'll become, because through your conversations, even if they're completely one-sided, she'll begin to understand language.

Step 2: Follow your instincts. You'll probably want to soften your voice and talk in a higher pitch than usual, and that's for good reason. Babies prefer it. Just remember to recalibrate your pitch and tone when you talk to your sweetie or answer the phone; otherwise, you'll annoy every adult within earshot.

Step 3: Relax. What you say matters less than that you say it, since your baby doesn't grasp the meaning of words quite yet. So pressure's off to come up with scintillating topics of conversation. Instead, just say whatever comes to mind. Tell her exactly what's happening when you're changing her diaper, getting her dressed, or walking down the street. With a little repetition, she'll start picking up on key words and, before you know it, repeating them back to you.

Step 4: Listen. Your baby will soon jump into the conversation, offering her own coos, a-goos, squeals, and even raspberries. When she does, smile and repeat whatever sound she makes back to her. Playing this game of call-and-response instills confidence in your baby by letting her know that you hear her, understand her, and will respond to her when she wants you to.

More Timeless Tips

- Got nothing to say? Try singing a song or reading a book.

- Look your baby in the eye when communicating with her. It'll turn your conversation into valuable bonding time, and you'll also be able to better read her signals. If she looks away (or, you know, starts howling), it may be time for some quiet. Come to think of it, the same holds true when you're talking to adults, too.

Get Giggles

. . .

"During infancy, your baby's brain is going the fastest it ever will, and you can be a parent who doesn't put much in it—or you can be somebody who deposits really great stuff."

—ROSEMARY GIUNTA

HOW TO PLAY GAMES

Step 1: Make funny noises. It's the low-hanging fruit on the humor tree. Form a seal between your mouth and his belly, thighs, arms, or feet, and blow. Zerberts are always good for a few smiles. And by about six months, so is the sound of ripping paper. (Search for it on YouTube if you don't believe it.)

Step 2: Build suspense. Make eye contact with your baby and let him know that you're going to kiss him like crazy very, very, *very* soon. Then make exaggerated steps toward him and deliver on your promise. Another option: Grab each of his toes, one by one, and recite this nursery rhyme:

This little piggy went to market.
This little piggy stayed home.
This little piggy had roast beef.
This little piggy had none.
And this little piggy went "Wee! Wee! Wee!" all the way home.

That last line is your cue to tickle him from toe to head.

Step 3: Play peekaboo. Note: This game is very different from the I'm-gonna-scare-the-crap-outta-you game. The idea is not to startle but to simply disappear and then reappear. Hold your hands in front of your face and open them. Peek overtop your newspaper (or your laptop, if you read the news like a normal person). Pop through a doorway. He'll be thrilled by the attention—and the surprise.

Step 4: Just be plain silly. You can turn just about anything into a game. Pull a tissue out of the box, throw it in the air, and hop all around, trying to catch it. Lie on your back, fold your knees toward your chest, rest your baby on your shins (if he can hold his head up), and pretend he's an airplane. Do the robot. Make funny faces. Hold him in front of the mirror and wiggle your eyebrows. Fill your cheeks with air and let him squeeze it out. You'll find that anything that makes him laugh will also make you laugh, so play with wild abandon.

More Timeless Tips

- Play is not only fun for the baby, it's fun for you, too. Watching your cherub all day, no matter how cute he is, can be mind-numbingly dull if you let it be. Allow yourself to be goofy, and you'll both be happier for it.

- Laughter is good for your health, in part because it triggers the release of feel-good endorphins. Besides, it's just fun. Once you figure out what makes your baby belly laugh—ripping a piece of paper, saying "boing" over and over, making a kissing noise—you'll want to do it again and again.

Groove Out

. . .

"After my mom would sing a song, she'd raise a baby's hands overhead and say 'Toots 'n' up!' I have no idea where that came from, but I did it to my own kids, and my grandchildren, too. They love it!"

—CLAIRE BRIED

HOW TO HAVE A SING-ALONG

Step 1: Memorize a few songs, if you don't know them already. A few goodies:

The Itsy-Bitsy Spider

The itsy-bitsy spider went up the water spout.
Down came the rain, and washed the spider out.
Out came the sun, and dried up all the rain,
and the itsy-bitsy spider went up the spout again.

If You're Happy and You Know It

If you're happy and you know it, clap your hands
If you're happy and you know it, clap your hands
If you're happy and you know it, then your face will surely show it
If you're happy and you know it, clap your hands.

Repeat the verse, replacing "clap your hands" with "stomp your feet," then "shout hooray," then "do all three."

Little Bunny Foo Foo

Little Bunny Foo Foo,
Hopping through the forest,
Scooping up the field mice and boppin' 'em on the head.
Down came the good fairy
And she said:
"Little Bunny Foo Foo, I don't want to see you
Scooping up the field mice and boppin' 'em on the head.
I'll give you three chances,
And if you don't behave
I'll turn you into a goon!"
The next day . . .

Repeat the verse, until Little Bunny Foo Foo runs out of chances. Then say,

I gave you three chances
And you didn't behave.
Poof!
Now you're a goon!

Step 2: Add hand motions. Capture your little one's attention, and imagination, by animatedly acting out each verse. Walk that itsy-bitsy spider up the spout with your fingers. *Be happy and know it*. Work those bunny ears.

Step 3: Repeat ad infinitum.

More Timeless Tips

- If you forget the words or, after your tenth rendition, you find the songs a touch predictable, make up your own lyrics. Your baby just wants to hear you sing and watch you dance. She's not listening for content quite yet.

- Don't worry if you're off-key. You're going for some laughs, not a record deal.

Be Handy

• • •

HOW TO MAKE SHADOW PUPPETS

Step 1: Find a good spot. You should be between a light or sunny window and a bare wall.

Step 2: Unleash your menagerie, using your hands and imagination.

- A bunny: You already know this one. Hold your right hand in the air, extend your pointer and middle finger, and tuck your ring finger and pinky in your palm under your thumb.

- A horse: Hold your right hand up, thumb pointing upward, pressing your ring and middle fingers together and your ring finger and pinky together. Make a gun-shape with your left hand, thumb up, pointer extended and slightly bent, and press it against the top of your right palm.

- A swan: Hold your left arm up as if you're about to show off your bicep, but turn your hand away from you and pinch your fingers and thumb together. Place your right hand, fingers splayed, in the crook of your elbow.

Step 3: Tell a story. Move your shadow animals all around and make all the funny noises that go with them. Bet you didn't know butterflies make noises. Well, technically they don't, but yours should. Your baby will love it.

More Timeless Tips

- You may find your baby is more interested in your hands than the shadows they cast. No matter, you're still putting on a good show.

Have Cake (and Eat It, Too)

. . .

"Parties today with all that fanfare? Forget it, lady. I've never heard of such a thing. What happened to fun and games? What happened to musical chairs? We had everlasting birthday parties from age one to ten. Oh boy. We'd buy all the kids kites and fly them on Randall's Island. And the adults had a good time, too, because we brought a bottle of wine."

—SUNCHITA TYSON

HOW TO PLAN A FIRST BIRTHDAY PARTY

Step 1: Set the date. The party doesn't have to be on your babe's exact birthday, especially if her lucky day falls somewhere in the middle of the week or on a holiday. Besides, she won't know the difference anyway. Heaps of attention and a piece of cake make for a good day, any day. In fact, that rule holds true throughout life. Also, keep in mind that your baby will probably get a few shots at her one-year checkup, which may leave her feeling under the weather for a few days afterward. So if you're split on when to have her party—before or after the big day—choose before (or way after).

Step 2: Set the time. You want your guest of honor to be happy, right? So plan the start and end times of the fiesta around her naps, and don't let the party drag on forever. An hour or two is just right.

Step 3: Choose the location. For wee ones, home is best. Not only is it the least expensive option, but it's also the place where she'll be most comfortable. You want her to be stimulated, of course, but too much excitement can lead to a meltdown. Also, hosting the shindig on your own turf means you can focus on the party and not on lugging her diaper bag, car seat, toys, and anything else along with you.

Step 4: Choose your colors. Your little one is (thankfully) probably too young to care about what her birthday plates look like. So make it easy on yourself and rather than choosing an actual theme, just stick with a color scheme, like yellow and aqua or lime green and orange. That way, it'll still feel festive, but you won't have to knock yourself out running to three different stores looking for those darn Elmo napkins.

Step 5: Invite the guests. About a month before the big day, send out invitations or e-mail or call your peeps. Rather than invite every single one of your Facebook friends who've ever "liked" a baby picture you've posted, keep the gathering limited to your innermost circle. Your baby will enjoy the day more, and your friends and colleagues can see the highlights online later.

Step 6: Plan the food. Everyone's there to celebrate your baby, not to partake in a seven-course tasting menu. So keep your eats simple. If the party takes place over a mealtime, grill burgers and dogs, order pizzas, or set up a build-your-own sandwich station. If not, put out plenty of snacks, like veggies and dip, fruit and cheese, and chips and pretzels. (Just be sure no little pieces fall on the floor, where they may present a choking hazard to your baby and any other young guests.) You'll also need drinks, of course. Think juice, soda, seltzer, milk, and if you'd like, wine and beer for the adults.

Step 7: Choose your decorations. You can't go wrong with colorful bunches of tulips, dahlias, or gerbera daisies, plunked into old Mason jars and set around the house; Mylar balloons (latex ones, if deflated or popped, present a choking hazard for little ones); and streamers.

Step 8: Bake the cake. Traditional birthday cakes with buttercream frosting are, of course, divine, but they also contain your baby's weight in sugar. (OK, not really, but it'll sure seem like it when you see her bouncing off the walls after she eats a piece.) Consider opting for something slightly less sugary, like a carrot, apple, or zucchini cake. If you want icing, go for a cream-cheese frosting or whipped cream. Cupcakes work, too.

Step 9: Have fun! It's a party, after all.

More Timeless Tips

- You'll probably have your hands full, so enlist a trusted friend or relative, preferably one who doesn't have the reputation of cutting off everyone's head in photos or putting her thumb over the camera lens, to take pictures. That way, you'll be able to enjoy every moment without worrying about whether you caught it on film.

• Create a safe space on the floor, where your baby can play and crawl around during the party. You don't want to have to hold her (and she may not want to be held) for the entire thing, so make it easier for both of you.

• Try not to stress. This is a day when you, and your baby, should feel surrounded by love. That's it.

• No need to open presents while everyone watches. Just be sure to send thank-you cards later.

10

Remembering

. . .

*Live in the moment, but take a little time to record the
best ones, so you can savor them forever.*

Plant Seeds

...

"When Karen got a little bit older, she was in the backyard looking at the plum tree, which had one lovely little plum on it. She kept walking around and around that tree, and then she came inside and said, 'What is that tree?' I said, 'If you want it, you could have that tree. I'll give it to you.' Sure enough, she ran out there and ate that plum."

—BETTY HORTON

HOW TO PLANT A COMMEMORATIVE TREE

Step 1: Choose the right tree. You'll watch it grow year after year, and even after your baby grows up, goes off to college, and conquers the world, it'll still be standing in your yard, and whenever you sit underneath it, you'll think of the very year he was born. So, better make sure you pick a tree that'll thrive under your care. It should be strong enough to weather the hottest and coldest temperatures in your area, and all the sunshine and rain you may or may not get.

Step 2: Find a good spot. Look up, look down, look all around, and make sure your tree will have plenty of space to grow. Your tree, like your babe, may look small now, but it won't be for very long, so don't plant it right next to your house, directly under utility lines, or on top of underground cables. (Call your power company to find out where they run.)

Step 3: Dig a hole. A well-planted tree will grow faster and live longer than a poorly planted tree, so take care to do it right. Using a shovel, dig a big ol' bowl-shaped hole as deep as the tree's roots (or root ball) and about twice as wide. The hole will most certainly look bigger than you think it needs to be, but the roots need that extra room to grow. Don't slack on the digging.

Step 4: Measure up. Place your tree in the hole and see if it's deep enough. If it's just right, proceed to Step 5. If it's too deep, put some soil back. If it's too shallow, enlist your honey to finish up for you. After all, you just had a baby, which entitles you to sit back and sip lemonade for at least a few minutes.

Step 5: Position your tree. It should stand upright in the center of the hole. If your tree comes in a container, give the pot a few taps to gently remove it, being careful not to rip the trunk from the roots. If your tree comes with its roots wrapped in burlap, plunk the whole thing in the pit and carefully remove the burlap, along with any twine, wire, nails, or staples.

Step 6: Fill the hole. Replace the soil you removed, packing it down firmly around the roots. You'll want your tree pit to catch water, so make sure your tree grows from its deepest point. Then look for a little bulge at the base of your tree's trunk. It's called the root collar, and you want your soil to snuggle its bottom only. If you can't see your tree's collar, it may be planted too deep.

Step 7: Add water. Give the ground a good soak.

Step 8: Spread mulch (wood chips or bark) around your tree a couple of inches deep. It'll help keep the soil warm and moist, prevent weeds and erosion, and just make the whole thing look nice.

Step 9: Enjoy it with your baby. He may not be old enough to appreciate his very own tree yet, but he will be one day. This year, it'll provide shade for him while he naps. In ten years, it'll provide sturdy branches from which he can swing. In twenty years, he'll lean against it with his guitar in hand, as he tries to teach himself to play Woody Guthrie songs. In thirty years, maybe he'll even marry his true love beneath it. Here's to your littlest sapling, with great expectations.

More Timeless Tips

- To find the best trees for your area, enter your zip code at arborday.org and get all the information you've ever dreamed of. Better yet, join the Arbor Day Foundation for $10, and you'll receive ten free trees of your choice. Seriously.

- Water your tree once a week and prune only dead or broken branches.

- If you're planting a sapling with naked roots, remove any packaging and soak the roots in a bucket of water for up to six hours before planting.

Set a Record

. . .

"I kept baby books. I wrote down everything: their first words, first foods, first steps, and how much they weighed until six months. Every once in a while, I look through them now. They bring back a lot of memories."

—MARY HUFF

HOW TO MAKE A MEMORY BOOK

Step 1: Buy a blank photo album or scrapbook with acid-free archival pages, along with self-adhesive photo corners and a contrasting gel pen.

Step 2: Stand at the ready with your camera. Whenever Junior does something major for the first time—smiles, belly laughs, takes a bath, sits up, crawls, stands, tries pureed peas (and proudly spits them everywhere), swims—take a quick snapshot. It doesn't have to be perfect, either. Sometimes the slightest blurriness from your moving hand—it's hard to clap and snap at the same time—only adds to the charm.

Step 3: Print your special photos. Don't leave them in your camera or on your phone forever. Use an online photo service or hit the photo kiosk at the drugstore the next time you're out buying diapers. It takes less time than you think. Really.

Step 4: Mount the photos in the book. Using the photo corners, secure your photos to the page.

Step 5: Label the event. Write down "the first," along with the date. You will be so surprised to see how much your little one has grown from each milestone to the next.

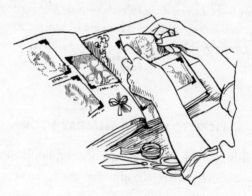

More Timeless Tips

- You can go as crazy as you'd like with this project, adding ribbons, borders, or whatever other scrapbooking bling-bling you'd like.

- If you miss *the* moment, don't fret. You can always sneak a photo of Baby's second steps, or third or fourth or fifth, into the album, and no one will know (or care). Besides, the consolation is pretty amazing: You've shared something beautiful with your baby without a camera coming between you, and while you may not have captured the milestone on film, it will most definitely still be seared into your memory forever.

- If you just can't find the time to print your photos right now, then at least back up your files in the meantime by copying them on an external hard drive or burning them onto a CD. You'll kick yourself (and probably cry a whole lot) if you lose your phone or camera and, along with it, every baby picture you ever took.

- If you fear you'll forget the dates of major events, jot them down on a piece of paper, along with a quick note, and drop them into a jar for future sorting.

Stow Away

. . .

*"I saved their hospital bands, a diaper, and their first preemie outfits,
which were too big at the time, just so I'd remember. Now they
look like dolly clothes. The things you want to save are things
that'll tell them something about themselves when they get bigger.
It's more for them than for you."*

—Erinn McGurn

HOW TO MAKE A KEEPSAKE BOX

Step 1: Buy a sturdy archival box and line it with acid-free archival paper.

Step 2: Toss in sentimental objects. Some ideas: her hospital bracelet, yours and your mate's, the ID card from her bassinet, the cap she wore in the hospital, a lock of hair, a newborn diaper (um, clean), her birth announcement, cards from well-wishers, any special photos, and whatever else strikes your fancy.

More Timeless Tips

- Remember, it's a box of keepsakes, not a filing cabinet. You don't have to save every last random item she ever touched, just the special stuff.

Dig Deep

· · ·

"We made a time capsule for Mario, and when we had a family gathering, everybody put something in it. My mother-in-law had cancer, and she didn't want anybody to see what she put in it. She died not too long after, and when we moved a few years later, we had to dig up the capsule. We said, 'Should we open it?' We did and she wrote a beautiful note to Mario, a thank-you for getting everybody together on that day."

—ROSEMARY GIUNTA

HOW TO MAKE A TIME CAPSULE

Step 1: Buy a time capsule. If you're actually going to bury it or you really do plan to save it for decades upon decades, choose one made of either aluminum, stainless steel, or, if you want to get all fancy-schmancy, copper. It should have either no seams or welded seams, and the end should be a screw top with a gasket. If you're not going to bury it but instead just pop it in your attic or closet, you might as well just get an archival box and line it with acid-free paper.

Step 2: Fill it with meaningful things, including:

- A copy of the front page of your local newspaper on the day your baby was born. Newsprint deteriorates in a snap, so photocopy it onto acid-free paper.

- Black-and-white pictures. Color prints will fade, even if they never see sunlight. Have your black-and-whites printed on fiber-based paper, so they last longer, and tuck each in an acid-free archival envelope with the image facing away from the seam.

- A recording of your baby cooing, talking, crying, even just breathing. Just make sure you either include the equipment needed for playback, or at least instructions on what kind of equipment is needed. It's hard to believe now, but maybe one day even iPods will go the way of the eight-track.

- Handwritten wishes from family members and close friends, slipped into polyethylene bags (available at archival supply stores).

- A letter to your baby (if he's the intended recipient).

- Whatever else marks this particular time in your life, and your baby's life.

Step 3: Seal it. No need to wield a welding torch, Flashdance. Just add a dab of two-part epoxy on the ends before screwing on the cap.

Step 4: Bag it. Drop your capsule in a six-millimeter polyethylene bag, which will offer a little extra protection from the elements.

Step 5: Bury it. Your hole needs to be at least three feet deep and preferably in a dry spot. Any shallower and the rise and fall of the ground temperature could ruin your treasures.

Step 6: Make a treasure map. Or at least write down the exact location where you buried the darn thing. As vivid as it is to you now, after thirty or more years, your memory might get a little fuzzy.

More Timeless Tips

- You might want to add one of those silica gel packs you find in shoe boxes and other random spots before sealing the capsule. It'll help keep any humidity in check.

- You'd be surprised how long his little cotton onesie will last. Cotton stores well, and so does polyester. Wool? Not so much. It'll eventually get gassy (tee-hee), which could corrode the metal.

- Never stow anything rubber. It'll break down and give off sulfur, which will muck up everything.

Stamp It

· · ·

*"I still have Asante's footprints, stamped in ink,
from when he was a baby. It brings back a lot of
memories. I can't believe that little foot went
on to win two Super Bowls."*

—Christine Samuel

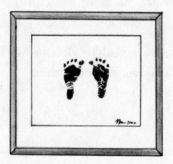

HOW TO FRAME FOOTPRINTS

Step 1: Gather your supplies. You'll need: a picture frame, several sheets of acid-free archival paper that fit the frame, and a stamp pad of nontoxic, washable ink.

Step 2: Recruit help. You'll need one person to hold the baby and another to do the stamping.

Step 3: Play rock, paper, scissors with your helper. The winner gets to hold the baby, while the loser can deal with the inky end of business.

Step 4: Get inked. Press your baby's feet, one at a time, into the stamp pad, making sure every toe and her heel are adequately coated.

Step 5: Panic a little bit. Try not to let her step on anything, including the floor, your pants, and oh my God, your beautiful white couch. Then, if only for a split second, ponder why you thought it was a good idea to buy a white couch right before you had kids.

Step 6: Take the print. Gently press her foot onto the center of the paper, making sure each toe hits the target and her sole flattens.

Step 7: Wash your baby. Use mild soap and water or baby oil to remove the ink.

Step 8: Frame the prints. Wait until they're dry, obviously.

More Timeless Tips

- Chances are you won't get a perfect print the first time out, so be patient and repeat it as often as necessary. If your baby is being a squirmy worm, table the project for another time or day.

- Like the footprints? Then do her hands next.

- If you don't want to use ink, you can also use nontoxic water-color paints. Just coat your baby's foot with the paint, barely touch her foot to a dish of water, then quickly and gently press it onto a piece of watercolor paper.

Seal It

. . .

"I started a journal when they were still in the NICU. It's written to them. It's important to me that when they're older, they understand how far they've come. I hope it'll give them confidence and I want them to know how strong they are and how proud I was of them even then."
—Erinn McGurn

HOW TO WRITE LETTERS TO YOUR BABY

Step 1: Gather your supplies. You'll need either some nice stationery with envelopes or a blank journal.

Step 2: Get all sentimental. Your relationship with your child will evolve over the years, and you may never get a chance to tell him everything you're thinking, feeling, wishing, and hoping for him. He doesn't understand you now, and before you know it, he'll be rolling his eyes at you when you try to tell him. But one day, maybe even when he becomes a parent himself, he'll want to know everything, and it'll be so sweet to tell him then.

Step 3: Write your letter. Address it to your child, date it, pour your heart out, and sign off.

Step 4: Stash it. If you're writing on stationery, seal your letter in an envelope, addressed to your child, and stow it in a box for safekeeping. If you're using a journal, simply shut the book and shelve it until you're ready to write again.

Step 5: Repeat Steps 1 through 4 as often as you feel moved.

Step 6: Wait about eighteen years. Or longer. Or less. It's up to you, but remember that the purpose of writing the letters is actually to give them to your child one day.

More Timeless Tips

- Prefer a high-tech version? Create an e-mail address for your child and shoot her a message whenever one comes to mind. One day, you can give her the password, and when she checks it, her inbox—and her heart—will be full.

Make an Impression

• • •

"I have Ronnie's handprint plate that we made together. It's something you can remember doing together, and you can show them and say, 'Look how little your hand was then!' It makes me want to cry, when I see his hand next to it now. They grow up so fast."

—MARY HUFF

HOW TO MAKE A HANDPRINT PLATE

Step 1: Gather your supplies. You'll need plaster of Paris, water, a bowl and spoon (for mixing), a disposable plate (paper, plastic, or aluminum), a straw, and a ribbon.

Step 2: Lay down old newspaper or paper bags to protect your work surface.

Step 3: Mix your plaster. Simply follow the manufacturer's instructions, making sure you use the kind of plaster that's safe on skin.

Step 4: Fill your mold. Any sort of disposable plate will do, as long as it's at least an inch deep.

Step 5: Do the deed. Once the plaster begins to set, usually within the first five minutes, gently press your baby's clean, dry hand into it, deep enough so it makes an impression, but not so deep that it hits the bottom. Hold it there for a minute, or at least until he looks like he's going to start squirming.

Step 6: Wash your baby's hand. Use a gentle baby soap and warm water.

Step 7: Make your ribbon hole at the top. Press a drinking straw (or pen cap or short dowel) into the plaster, so it hits the plate.

Step 8: Wait a day, until the plaster sets. Be patient. If you move too soon, you'll have to start over.

Step 9: Pop it out. Gently remove the plaster from the plate and then remove your straw (or pen cap or dowel) from the hole at the top.

Step 10: Add the ribbon. Thread it through the hole at the top and knot it off.

Step 11: Hang the plate in a prominent spot with pride.

More Timeless Tips

- Mix enough plaster to make a couple of molds, in case your babe decides he wants to grope the plate.

- If you'd like to add your child's name and the date, carve it in with a pencil between Steps 7 and 8.

- You can do footprints, too. If your baby is small enough, you may be able to fit both feet on one plate.

Cast Away

· · ·

*"I kept all of their first shoes. They're lined up on my bookcase; at our
Passover Seder, my youngest granddaughter walked over to them, picked
out her father's pair, and put them on. It was so sweet."*

—Esther Safran Foer

How to Bronze Baby Shoes

Step 1: Find the perfect place to display your baby shoes. Otherwise, after two days of this bronzing process, you'll begin to wonder why you started this kitschy, old-school project in the first place.

Step 2: Choose your baby shoes. Go for a pair your baby's already outgrown; otherwise, this craft will seem awfully mean.

Step 3: Gather your other supplies: You'll need cotton balls and swabs, denatured alcohol, rubber cement, plaster of Paris (and a mixing bowl and spoon), two tiny screws and a screwdriver or drill, two pieces of string, a varnish (like polyurethane or spar varnish), bronzing powder (available at hardware and art stores), a mixing cup, and a paintbrush.

Step 4: Fill the boots. Mix, then pour, plaster of Paris into each shoe, stopping about a half inch from the top. Put the booties in a safe place and wait twenty-four hours for the plaster to dry.

Step 5: Clean the shoes. Wipe them down thoroughly with a cotton ball or swab soaked with denatured alcohol. Wash the laces if you'd like, too.

Step 6: Arrange the laces. Tie them however you'd like, and use a few dabs of rubber cement to hold them in place.

Step 7: Add drying hooks. Because you'll need to hang your bronzed shoes to dry, screw a tiny screw into the bottom of each sole and tie a string around each.

Step 8: Bronze them. Mix your bronzing powder with your varnish, until it looks like paint. Then, using a soft paintbrush, slap it on the shoes.

Step 9: Hang to dry. Tie the other end of the strings you've screwed into the bottom of the shoes to a knob, pole, or tree branch and allow the bronze to dry.

Step 10: Display proudly. They'll be too heavy for your rear-view mirror, so find an empty table or something that needs just a touch of kitsch and nostalgia.

More Timeless Tips

- Stir your bronzing paint often, so the coppery particles remain evenly suspended throughout it.

- If you've missed any spots, you can always go back later and dab on more bronzing solution.

Say Cheese

. . .

*"My husband took a ton of pictures. The days seemed
interminable sometimes, which happens when you get tired and
the baby has lots of energy, but when you look back at the pictures,
you realize time goes so fast."*

—RUTH ALSOP

HOW TO START A BUNNY PROJECT

Step 1: Choose a fuzzy bubba. You know that adorable stuffed
bunny (or owl, bear, or whatchamacallit) you've been staring at in
the window of that baby store on the way home from your OB
appointment every week? Go buy it, and appreciate how fluffy it
is. In a few months, its fur will be lovingly matted with drool.
(Incidentally, that will only make you love it more.)

Step 2: Scout a location. Choose a spot in your home that's
simple, accessible, and clutter free, where you can sit, prop, or lay
your baby. Cushy chairs, chaise lounges, or beds work well.

Step 3: Take the picture. Beginning a week or so after your
baby is home, set her in her spot with her bunny at her side. At
first, she won't be able to sit up on her own, so you may have to
lean her on a pillow (with you standing inches away, of course, for
safety). Hold your camera at her eye level and snap away. Try to

capture all of her expressions—not just the smiles, but also the frowns, yawns, and furrowed brows.

Step 4: Repeat. Take another picture of her next to her bunny in the same spot on the same day every month. You won't notice how fast she's growing when you're looking at her every day, but when you compare these shots from month to month, you will be amazed.

More Timeless Tips

- Dress her in something simple, like a white onesie, that allows you to see her arms and legs. That way, you can count each additional thigh roll, wrist crease, and elbow dimple.

- Take a few close-ups to capture details and a few shots from farther away to capture perspective.

- Enlist your partner (or mom, sister, or friend) to help. One of you can shoot while the other watches and entertains the baby.

- The older she gets, the faster she's going to move when you put her down. Expect more than a few blurry pictures of her tush as she crawls away.

- Continue the project for the first year, sharing the photos with family and friends (in person or online) as you take them. Then frame all twelve pictures for her first birthday, so you'll have a record of her growth that first year.

- After the first year, make the Bunny Project an annual event on birthdays, not a monthly event, or your teenager will never forgive you.

Acknowledgments
...

Just as it takes loads of help to raise a child, it also takes loads of help to write a book. I owe big hugs and my sincere thanks:

To all the incredible mothers who shared their stories and wisdom with me. Especially Ruth Alsop of Saratoga Springs, New York, who inspired me with her strength; Rosemary Giunta of Hiawatha, Iowa, who really is a somebody; Betty Horton of Conneaut, Ohio, who welcomed me into her cottage and regaled me with tales of her long life on the eve of her 102nd birthday party; Mary Huff of Erie, Pennsylvania, who showed me what it means to be generous; Elaine Maddow of Castro Valley, California, who not only reminded me that your best actually is good enough but also never once hung up the phone without asking about my daughter; Erinn McGurn of Brooklyn, New York, who is as great a friend as she is a mother; Esther Safran Foer of Washington, D.C., who reminded me that your intuition will never fail you; Christine Samuel, who taught me about perseverance; and Toni Tyson of North Salem, New York, who, as I discovered while sitting on her porch one summer afternoon, is as open and friendly as she is impressive. I feel honored to have had the opportunity to learn from each of you.

To my own mom, Claire Bried of Orefield, Pennsylvania, who probably taught me more about what it means to be a mother than anyone else. Thank you for all the love, guidance, and help.

To my editors, Jill Schwartzman, for always believing in me, and Christine Pride, for your support, warmth, and enthusiasm; and all my new friends at Hyperion, including Ellen Archer, Elisabeth Dyssegaard, Kristin Kiser, Marie Coolman, Kristina Miller, Bryan Christian, and Sam O'Brien.

To the pros who read the manuscript, including pediatricians Dr. Erin Meyer and Dr. Lauren Henning, as well as certified child-birth educator and postpartum doula Laura Tichler. Thank you for your friendly advice and expert eyes.

To Holly Bemiss, my literary agent and first reader. Thank you for helping me find that word I was thinking of again and again and again. I don't know what I'd ever do without you.